the

HERB COOKERY

100 recipes and 200 uses

This book formerly published by the Herb Purveyor.
This revised edition is published by Father & Son Publishing, Inc.

ISBN: 0-942407-46-6

05 04 03 02 01 00 99/10 9 8 7 6 5 4

Published
by

FATHER&SON
PUBLISHING, INC.
4909 North Monroe Street
Tallahassee, Florida 32303
800-741-2712
http://www.fatherson.com
e-mail lance@fatherson.com

INTRODUCTION

During my years of herbal farming I met so many people who wanted to know how to use and grow herbs. I hope this book will be useful in addressing both requests. Herbs are so resourceful, so giving and so universal in their appeal and usage that there are no boundaries for continued knowledge. They enrich everyone's life by bringing joy and delight through taste, touch, aroma and health. This book attempts to share my knowledge and experience with you and to bring you a glimpse of the bounty we have been given. I hope it will encourage you to learn more about these fascinating and glorious gifts with which we have been so graciously blessed.

DEDICATION

This book is dedicated to my Mother,
Dorothy Macy Frush, who introduced me to the
joys and wonder of gardening and the pleasure
and responsibility of caring for the earth.

ACKNOWLEDGEMENTS

Special thanks to my Dad, Richard Frush, who taught me that dreams are a prelude to reality and for his many years of experience he shared so patiently with me.

To my daughter, Jocelyn, who was there to help during the worst and best times, allowing the dream to continue.

To my son, Richard, whose belief in me sustained me through hardships and whose own courage inspired greater efforts from me.

To my sister and brother-in-law, Audrey and Willy Fitch, who gave of their time when called.

To Cathy Smith whose friendship and council have always been cherished and whose eye for detail helped in editing this book.

To my many friends and neighbors who were there when all could have been lost and rejoiced when it wasn't. Especially to Dot Joyner, Bill Ingram, O. L. Warren, Kathy Carney, Wyth Thompson and Lewis Moren.

To Ann Wilson — On The Gallery, Crystal Beach, Texas, 77650 — for such beautiful and loving illustrations.

TABLE OF CONTENTS

Barbara Scoggins Frush has been growing herbs commercially for 16 years. She started growing for Dallas, Texas restaurants and up-scale grocery stores in 1985 and grew the business to 30 restaurants and 115 grocery stores by 1991. She was a member of the Texas Organic Growers Association and on the board of the Herb Growers and Marketing Association of Texas. She left Texas and founded another company in Chicago, selling her fresh cut herbs from organic farms to 55 restaurants and 279 grocery stores in the greater Chicago area. Planning to semi-retire, Barbara sold this business and returned to Galvaston, Texas where she opened a Bed and Breakfast in an historical home. There she developed herbal food products for retail and restaurant sale and offered *High Tea* on Wednesdays and on garden tours throughout the year. After three fulfilling years, she moved to South Miami and has begun another herb business to incorporate her love and knowledge of herbs with her love for cooking and sharing with others. Check out her website @ www.herbalgourmet.com and enjoy organic foods from around the world and her own kitchen. **The Herb Cookery** reflects her knowledge gained from many years of experience and sharing with some of the most famous chefs in this country. Enjoy, learn and use.

Culinary
Use

CULINARY USE INDEX

For fully cross-referenced index, see page 83.

ARUGULA   Although not a true herb, arugula's usage has become synonymous with herbal cooking and for that reason it is found in the fresh herb section of the grocers. Arugula has a wide slightly scalloped leaf that resembles a radish in taste and aroma. The taste is a welcome change in salads, sauces and pastas. Arugula can only be used fresh.

BASIC ARUGULA SALAD

6   leaves of arugula, torn in bite size pieces

2   cups of Bibb lettuce

2   cups of red oak lettuce

1/2   cup of tarragon vinaigrette or any oil and vinegar dressing

Toss all ingredients together 30 times. Serve at room temperature. Serves 2.

ARUGULA AND MELON SALAD

2   cups of arugula leaves, washed and torn

1   honeydew melon, the meat cut into cubes

1/4   cup of diced chicken

1/2   orange

1   teaspoon lime juice

Sea salt and pepper to taste

In a large bowl, combine the first 4 ingredients, tossing with wooden spoons until thoroughly mixed. In a small bowl combine the next 2 ingredients and stir with a fork until well blended. Pour the dressing over the salad and toss 30 times with wooden spoons. Serves 2. Pine nuts or walnuts could be added.

ARUGULA WITH PASTA

1	pound pasta seashells, cooked al dente	1/3	cup olive or basil oil
2	cups of torn arugula leaves	1/3	cup of diced Calamati olives
3	cloves of garlic, minced	1/2	cup of freshly grated Asiago or Romano cheese

Toss the pasta in the oil until the pasta is well blended and the oil is absorbed. In a bowl, mix the arugula, garlic, olives and cheese together. Mix the arugula mixture in with the pasta, tossing with wooden spoons. Serve warm or cold. Serves 4.

BRAISED ARUGULA SAUCE

1/4 cup olive oil
3 cups of shredded arugula leaves

2 cloves of garlic, sliced thin
1/2 teaspoon thyme

In a heavy skillet, heat the oil until quite hot but not smoking. Stir in the next three ingredients until the arugula is crispy. Serve over grilled pork chops. Makes enough for 4 servings.

ARUGULA AND ARTICHOKES

1 can artichoke hearts, reserve juice
1/2 cup arugula leaves, torn

1 tablespoon lemon juice
Sea salt and pepper to taste

In a pan, heat the artichokes and arugula in the artichoke juice until arugula is limp. Add lemon juice and salt and pepper to taste. Serve hot as a side dish or add an herb mayonnaise and serve cold. Serves 4.

BASIL

BASIL For centuries people have been relying on various types of basil not only to enhance their cooking, but also to ward off evil spirits, soothe tired bodies, relieve stomach aches and frayed nerves. It's no wonder that these beautiful, aromatic and delicious herbs are so popular. Fresh basil is recommended and is always added to the recipe at the last five minutes. There are ways of preserving the fresh taste. Fresh chopped basil may be frozen and although the leaves will turn black, the taste is left intact. Use frozen, just putting it directly into the sauce or soup during cooking. Another even better way is to put 1 cup of leaves in a food processor, add just enough oil to form a paste. Put in an air tight container and store in the refrigerator. Spoon out the desired amount, using the same measurement as called for in the recipe. The paste will keep up to six months. Basil can be dried but much of the taste is lost. There are many different types of basil, the following being the most widely used:

SWEET BASIL is the best known basil and is used in Italian, Mediterranean and Thai cooking. Because of its slightly clove taste it blends with pestos, tomato sauces, soups, stews, cheeses, poultry, beans and vegetables.

OPAL BASIL is a dark purple plant with smooth or ruffled leaves. It is more aromatic than sweet basil and has a lighter, more minty quality. Opal basil is ideal added to pizza, plain or creamed pastas, chicken or shrimp salads, in vinegars and/or marinades for poultry, pork and shrimp.

LEMON BASIL is a much more delicate plant with smallish leaves and a distinctive lemon fragrance and taste. An excellent choice for seafood, poultry, salads, vegetables, desserts and tea.

ANISE BASIL is similar in appearance to the broad leaf sweet basil but the licorice fragrance alerts you to the difference. The addition of the licorice or tarragon-like flavor makes it a favorite in the southern regions of the Mediterranean.

STUFFED ARTICHOKE HEARTS

1 pound cream cheese	3 ounces Parmesan cheese (reserve
4 ounces fresh basil	1 ounce for later)
1 ounce garlic	Sea salt and white pepper to taste
1/2 teaspoon Worcestershire sauce	2 cans quartered artichokes

Blend well the first five ingredients. Stuff the artichokes with a generous amount of the cream cheese mixture. Broil for 10 - 15 minutes or until cheese mixture is creamy. Top with the remaining Parmesan cheese and serve with garlic toasted rounds or toasted bagel chips. Makes 16 - 20 hearts.

Recipe from David A. Beehler, Executive Chef,
Mere Bulles Restaurant in Nashville, Tennessee

COOL SUMMER SALAD

2 avocados, diced	2 cloves of minced garlic
1 tomato, diced	3 tablespoons olive oil
1 4-ounce jar marinated artichokes, diced	1 tablespoon tarragon vinegar
4 teaspoons chopped or minced fresh sweet basil (or 6 teaspoons lemon basil)	1/2 tablespoon lemon juice

Combine first 5 ingredients. Toss with wooden spoon so as not to bruise avocado. Combine the oil, vinegar and lemon in a small bowl and whisk until completely blended. Pour over salad and toss for 20 - 25 times. Chill in the refrigerator for 20 minutes. Serves two for lunch or four appetizers.

SPAGHETTI SQUASH WITH BASIL & OREGANO

1/3 cup fresh minced sweet basil
(or 1/2 cup of opal basil)

1 tablespoon fresh minced oregano

1 tablespoon fresh minced rosemary

3 tablespoons fresh grated Parmesan
cheese

2 cloves of fresh minced garlic
Sea salt and fresh black pepper
to taste

3 tablespoons olive oil

2 pounds spaghetti squash

Cut the squash in half. Place cut side down in a deep pan. Pour 1/2 cup water into pan and simmer for approximately 30 minutes or until squash is tender. (Squash can be placed in a glass pan with 1/4 cup water and covered with plastic wrap. Place in microwave on high for 12 minutes.) In a bowl, combine the first six ingredients until thoroughly blended. When squash is cooled slightly, take a fork and scrape the inside of the squash to form spaghetti-like strands. Toss the squash in the basil sauce until well blended. Top with additional Parmesan if desired. Serve with mixed salad and good garlic bread. Serves 2.

PESTO MERE BULLES

Pesto:

4 ounces minced sweet basil

2 ounces fresh grated garlic

4 ounces walnuts

2 ounces olive oil

2 ounces fresh Parmesan cheese
Sea salt and white pepper to taste

Pasta:

1 pound fresh pasta, seashells or
curly, cooked al dente

1 cup whipping cream

1 pound shrimp, diced

1 pound scallops, quartered

1 cup dry white wine

Prepare pesto by combining all ingredients except walnuts in a blender until pureed. Add walnuts until well blended. Braise shrimp and scallops in one tablespoon olive oil until shrimp are pink and scallops are completely white — about 3-4 minutes. Add cream, white wine along with pesto to the pasta. Toss well and serve immediately.

Presented by David A. Beebler, Executive Chef,
Mere Bulle Restaurant, Nashville, Tennessee

PRIMA VERA

2   ounces extra-virgin olive oil

A total of two cups of:

Julienne carrots

Julienne zucchini (just the outer
layer)

Julienne yellow squash (just the
outer layer)

Green peas

Diced fresh asparagus

Broccoli flowerettes

Diced Roma tomatoes

1/2   cup fresh spinach

3/4   tablespoon fresh chopped garlic

2   ounces dry white wine

1/4   cup fresh chopped basil, sweet or
opal

1   tablespoon whole butter or
margarine

Salt and white pepper

Here is your chance to get a little creative. Leave out vegetables you do not
like. Add some more that you do like (mushrooms, English peas, and snow
peas work well). Avoid long cooking vegetables such as green beans, Brussels
sprouts or cauliflower. Adjust the ratios according to your wishes. You are the
one eating and no one knows better than you what you like. I do recommend
avoiding vegetables with strong earthy tastes since they will overpower the
flavor of the basil, sauce and other vegetables.

Heat a large skillet, sauté pan or wok on a high flame. Before the pan gets too
hot, add the olive oil. Add all the vegetables except tomatoes and spinach.
Lightly sauté 1-1 1/2 minutes. Add tomatoes and garlic and season with salt
and white pepper. Sauté another 1 1/2 minutes. Add wine and fresh basil.
Sauté another minute and add whole butter. When melted, toss with fresh
spinach and cooked basil fettuccine. This will make one serving.

*From Scotty Griffey, the Executive Chef at
Flip's Wine Bar, Dallas, Texas*

❖ Over your favorite large pizza, mince 1/2 cup of opal or sweet basil just
after you bring it out of the oven.

❖ Add a teaspoon of fresh minced sweet, lemon or opal basil to 1 cup of
cooked vegetables just before serving.

❖ Add a teaspoon of fresh minced anise basil to any cooked fish.

LEMON BASIL CHICKEN

1/3 cup minced lemon basil	1/4 cup tarragon or rosemary vinegar
1 clove garlic, minced	2 tablespoons olive oil
Sea salt and white pepper to taste	2 chicken breasts, skinned and boned

Combine the first 5 ingredients and whisk well until thoroughly blended. Add chicken breasts and marinate for four to five hours in the refrigerator. Chicken may be oven broiled, pan broiled or grilled, using the marinade mixture as a baste. Cook approximately 15 minutes or until a fork inserted into the thickest part releases a clear white fluid when withdrawn. Serves two. (For a different taste, change the lemon basil to opal basil or anise basil).

BASIL VINEGAR

1 16 ounce amber jar	16 ounces distilled white vinegar
Approximately 1 pound of fresh basil—opal, anise or sweet	

Stuff basil into jar, macerating with a wooden spoon after 1/2 has been added. When jar is full of basil, macerate again to bruise the basil still further. Add vinegar, secure lid very well and set the jar in a sunny window. Every day turn the bottle over, for two weeks. Decant the vinegar into jars and store in a cool, dark area until ready to use. The vinegar will be strong and flavorful. Use as a marinade, salad dressing, or in sauces.

BASIL BUTTER

1 stick butter, room temperature	1/3 cup minced basil — any of the basils will do, each will impart a different taste

Place the butter and the minced basil in a blender or food processor and puree. Put in an airtight container and store in the refrigerator. Use on grilled meats, in cooked vegetables of all kinds, as a spread on sandwiches or toast and in some desserts as a substitute for plain butter or shortening.

CHIVES
Culpepper thought this plant was a poison to the brain but most chefs today wouldn't cook without it. Chives were first used in the Far East and brought to the Mediterranean around the 5th century. Chives are a welcome addition to most any dish. The pink to mauve flowers are very flavorful and can be added anywhere chives are used. Chives may be frozen and chopped directly into soups, stews, etc. They do not dry well.

GARLIC CHIVES are a favorite of mine. They are much larger than regular chives and have flat leaves and an umbel of small white flowers in the fall. Their light garlic taste enhances the flavor and depth of any dish. A special treat for anyone who likes garlic.

CHIVE-PIMENTO SPREAD

1/2 cup cream cheese, softened
1/3 cup minced chives

1/3 cup chopped pimentos, drained

Combine all ingredients until thoroughly blended. Put in the refrigerator for two hours. Serve over warm toast points, bagel chips, or whole wheat rolls. Try substituting cottage cheese for a slightly different flavor and texture.

CHIVE BUTTER SAUCE

1   stick butter
3   tablespoons chopped chives or
      garlic chives
2   tablespoons chopped Italian
      parsley

1   tablespoon lemon
      Sea salt and white pepper to taste

In a heavy saucepan, combine all ingredients and stir until completely blended and thickened. Use as a baste for broiled chicken or fish. (Add twice the lemon if used over fish.) Also good in vegetables.

CHIVE SUMMER SALAD

2 cucumbers, diced	Sea salt and black pepper to taste
1 cup cherry tomatoes, halved	4 tablespoons olive oil
1 avocado, diced	2 tablespoons basil vinegar
1/2 cup feta cheese, crumbled	1 tablespoon lemon juice
1/4 cup Greek olives (Calamati) or	2 tablespoon basil — opal or sweet,
Spanish olives	minced
1/4 cup chopped chives	

In a large bowl, combine first 7 ingredients. In a separate cup, whisk together the next 4 ingredients. Pour dressing over salad, toss 30 times and refrigerate for 1 hour. If desired, serve over Bibb or sorrel lettuce. Makes 2 luncheon salads.

CHIVE/MUSTARD BUTTER

1/4 cup mustard—the coarser the better	1 stick butter, softened
3 tablespoons vinegar—wine	4 tablespoons chopped chives — or
vinegar can be substituted	substitute 3 tablespoons chopped
3/4 teaspoon sea salt	garlic chives
1/2 teaspoon sugar	

In a heavy saucepan, mix together the first four ingredients. Gradually add the butter and whisk over low flame until sauce has reached a creamy consistency. Remove from heat and stir in the chives. Pour into serving bowl. Use on roasts of all kinds or over green beans, broccoli, spinach or baked onions.

❖ Chives in scrambled eggs are a welcome visual and culinary change. Add 1 tablespoon minced chives per egg and enjoy the difference.

GARLIC CHIVE POTATOES

1	pound new potatoes, quartered with the skin left on	1/2	cup buttermilk
2	tablespoons butter	1/2	cup cream
2	garlic cloves, minced	1	cup Montrachet cheese, crumbled
2	scallions, diced fine	1/4	cup garlic chives, minced
			Sea salt and black pepper to taste

Place the potatoes in a large pot with enough water to cover. Boil for 30 minutes or until potatoes are done, drain and set aside. In a heavy saucepan, melt the butter, add the scallions and garlic and cook for 15 minutes. Add the next three ingredients, stirring constantly. When the mixture has thickened, add the chives and season with salt and pepper. Pour over the potatoes and serve. Serves 4 - 6.

❖ In all soups, stews, chowders add 1/4 cup of fresh minced chives to 2 cups cooked soup. Add chives just before serving.

❖ Place whole strips of garlic chives in sandwiches for a refreshing difference.

DILL

This lovely lacy leaved plant is a great friend in the kitchen. Dill *leaves* are wonderful in dumplings, pasta or rice dishes, over salmon, shrimp or tuna. Dill *seeds* are rubbed into lamb, chicken and pork and used in soups, stews, condiments and sauces. Dill *vinegar* adds to the flavor of warm potato salad, cream cheese, cauliflower and cabbage, To retain the flavor of fresh dill, freeze dill leaves and add them frozen to the recipe. Dill dries well and can be kept in an airtight jar for about three months. To store dill seeds refer to the chapter on Cultivation. Dill seeds can be kept in an airtight container and stored in the refrigerator. They will keep for a year.

DILL SAUCE

1   cup plain yogurt
3   tablespoons fresh minced dill
1 1/2   teaspoons Dijon mustard

2   tablespoons capers, optional
1   tablespoon lemon juice

Mix all ingredients together. Chill for four hours. Serve with broiled white fish fillets, or toss with grilled shrimp, or add to 2 cups of cold diced cucumbers, or heat and serve over thin slices of roast pork or veal. Makes 1 cup.

DILLED DUMPLINGS WITH GRAVY

2   tablespoons butter
1/4 cup chopped fresh dill
1   tablespoon baking powder

2   cups flour
3/4 cup buttermilk
4   cups chicken stock

Place butter and flour in food processor with dill and baking powder and process for three minutes. Transfer to mixing bowl and add buttermilk and mix until dough forms. Knead on floured surface for 4 minutes. Form dough into 1 ounce balls. Bring chicken stock to a boil, reduce heat until chicken stock is just under a boil and poach dumplings for 4 minutes.

From Executive Chef Paul Brenholt,
Deep Ellum Cafe, Inc., Dallas, Texas

SUMMER DILL SOUP WITH AVOCADOS AND CUCUMBERS

3   large cucumbers, peeled and
    chopped
2   sweet onions, peeled and finely
    chopped
3   garlic cloves, minced
1   tablespoon sesame oil or vegetable
    oil
3   cups chicken stock—vegetable
    stock may be substituted

2   small ripe avocados or 1 large
    California avocado
1/3 cup minced fresh dill—have extra
    sprigs for garnish
1   cup heavy cream
    Sea salt and white pepper to taste

In a heavy, large pot sauté cucumbers, onions and garlic in hot oil until onions are soft and transparent. Stir in stock, reduce heat and simmer for 15 minutes. Pour 1/2 of mixture into a food processor or blender and blend until very smooth. Add 1/2 avocado to this mixture and continue to blend. Do the remaining 1/2 the same way. Return all of the soup to a large bowl—straining if necessary. Stir in the dill. Cover the bowl and place in the refrigerator for 6-8 hours. When ready to serve, stir in the cream and place some whole dill sprigs on top of each serving. White pepper and sea salt may be added at this time. Serves 4.

DILLED SHRIMP

1/3 cup butter
3   cloves garlic, minced
1   pound large shrimp, shelled and
    deveined

1/3 cup dill, minced
2   tablespoons lemon juice, or white
    wine may be substituted

In heavy skillet, melt the butter, add the garlic and stir until garlic is softened. Add the shrimp and stir until the skin turns pink, quickly add the dill and lemon juice and stir until blended. Serve over rice or by itself with a salad and crusty bread. Serves 4.

ZUCCHINI AND DILLED TOMATO PASTA

3 large zucchini, cubed

2 tablespoons sesame oil or vegetable oil

1 cup of stewed tomatoes

1 12-ounce package of macaroni or small shells, cooked al dente

Sea salt and black ground pepper to taste

1/4 cup fresh minced dill

In heavy skillet, sauté the zucchini in hot oil for approximately 10 minutes, stirring occasionally. Add the next two items and stir until well blended and hot. Add salt and pepper to taste. Add dill and serve. Makes a great side dish with chicken or braised meat or a light dinner with an arugula salad, good country bread and smoked Gouda. Serves 4 - 6.

DILL VINEGAR

1 8-ounce amber jar

1/2 pound fresh dill

1 cup distilled white vinegar

In jar, stuff at least 1/2 pound of fresh dill, macerating with a wooden spoon to release more of the flavor. Cover with vinegar, securing the lid very tightly. Place the jar in a sunny window and turn the jar upside down every day for two weeks. Decant and keep in the refrigerator. Use in salad dressings, over vegetables—hot or cold, as a marinade for salmon, tuna or chicken, over cucumbers or tomatoes and seafood pasta dishes.

❖ Put fresh minced dill over sauerkraut and sausages just before serving.

❖ Place minced dill over cottage cheese to brighten and "cool" the taste.

❖ When serving a New England style dinner, put minced dill over the cooked cabbage and other vegetables.

❖ Add 1 teaspoon dill to 1 cup clam chowder.

EDIBLE FLOWERS have become very popular

and are used not only for their visual complement but for the robust flavors they add. All of the herbs in this book except tarragon produce a flower which is edible and can be substituted for the herb in the recipe. The visual effect of a cascade of snapdragons or sweetpeas on a pound cake or the addition of calendula or nasturtium flowers in a summer salad make the meal a special and memorable occasion. Listed below are other edible flowers that you can grow and use in your recipes. Let your imagination be as open as the flowers are colorful.

Borage
Daisy—English or Ox-eye
Dandelion
Daylilies
Elderberry
Impatiens
Honeysuckle
Johnny-jumpups
Nasturtiums

Pansy
Pinks, carnations, dianthus
Rose and rose-hips
Squash blossoms—especially the Sardane variety
Violets
Snapdragon
Sweet pea

NOTE: Edible flowers should always be organically grown and not have been sprayed with any chemicals after cutting.

MARIGOLD Because of its unique and versatile qualities, marigold deserves individual treatment. Calendula Officinal is the variety most recommended for culinary use. Although it doesn't have a great deal of fragrance, its brilliant 3-inch orange and yellow flowers more than compensate. The name is derived from calender because this variety will bloom almost year round. The flowers are added whole or as petals to soups, stews, salads, sauces, roasts, cream cheese, risottos and pasta. The young leaves have a peppery taste and are welcome in salads, cream soups, poultry and fish. The petals are recommended as a substitute for saffron.

LEMON MARIGOLD POUND CAKE WITH LEMON DRIZZLE ICING

Your favorite pound cake recipe

3 tablespoons lemon juice

6 tablespoons organically raised marigold petals (the calendula variety)

To your favorite pound cake, add 6 tablespoons of organically raised marigold (calendula) petals and lemon juice. Blend into batter and cook according to directions.

Lemon Drizzle Icing

1 cup powdered sugar

1/4 cup of lemon juice

4-6 yellow and gold calendula flowers

In a mixing bowl, blend the sugar and lemon juice — to make a sauce-like consistency. Pour over top of cooled pound cake; cut the flowers in fourths and decorate.

ROSE AND FRUIT SALAD

1/4 pound of organically raised rose petals

3 large ripe bananas

1 cup golden currants

1 cup chopped dates

1 cup of fruit conserve — specialty stores

2 oranges, squeezed, and the juice set aside

1/2 cup crème fraîche or home made whipping cream

In a crystal or glass bowl, place the rose petals in a single layer on the bottom and sides. In a mixing bowl, mash the bananas, and add the currants and dates, until well blended. Cover the petals with this mixture. Next spread the conserve over the layer of date mixture. Let sit in the refrigerator for at least 4 hours. When ready to serve, pour the juice from the two oranges over the conserve and then cover with the crème fraîche or whipping cream. Serve immediately.

BORAGE SANDWICHES

8 ounces cream cheese, room
   temperature

1/4 cup borage flowers and young
     leaves, chopped (cucumber-like
     taste)
4   slices bread with crusts removed

Combine first 2 ingredients in a bowl, spread 1/4 on each slice of bread. Cut each slice into halves, forming two triangles per slice. Serve open-faced.

NASTURTIUM SALAD

1/2 cup arugula leaves
1   cup sorrel leaves
1   cup baby Bibb lettuce
1   cup nasturtium flowers, chopped

1/4 cup basil vinegar
1/2 cup garlic oil or balsamic oil
     Sea salt and freshly ground black
     pepper

In a large bowl, tear all of the lettuce leaves into bite size pieces. Toss in the chopped flowers. Mix together the oil and vinegar, whisking well; drizzle over the salad, add sea salt and fresh ground black pepper to taste. Toss 30 times and serve. Makes 4 servings.

STUFFED SQUASH BLOSSOMS

20 squash blossoms
2   tablespoons butter, melted
8   ounces small curd cottage cheese,
    drained

1/4 cup pine nuts
1/4 cup Parmesan cheese
     Sea salt and pepper to taste

In a bowl, combine all ingredients but the blossoms. Place 1 tablespoon of the stuffing mixture into each blossom, carefully tucking the ends to avoid leakage. Place blossoms in a shallow pan and drizzle the butter over them. Bake at 350°F for 15 minutes. Makes 4 - 6 servings.

❖ Flowers can always be used as garnish, but try them in sauces, soups and dessert icings as well as salads and teas.

LAVENDER is one of the best known herbs and is grown

primarily for its famous aroma and lovely mauve flowers. Lavender has become synonymous with youthful appearance, gracious living and peaceful surroundings. In the kitchen, lavender flowers are a wonderful addition to dessert sauces, vinegars, jellies, fruit salads, ice cream and as a garnish with lamb, poultry and pork. Lavender can be dried by hanging bundles of cut stems upside down in a closet or garage for 2 - 3 weeks. When completely dry, remove flowers and leaves storing separately in airtight containers.

LAVENDER DESSERT SAUCE

1   cup lavender flowers, finely   1   cup water
    chopped   1/2 cup sugar

In a heavy saucepan, boil the sugar and water until the sugar dissolves. Reduce the heat and add the lavender. Simmer, partially covered, for one hour, adding to the water if necessary. Cool slightly and pour through a sieve. Store in the refrigerator. This is especially good over ice cream, raisin pudding, or pound cake. Garnish with additional lavender flower heads. Makes 3/4 cup.

LAVENDER MEAT SAUCE

1   tablespoon flour   1/2 cup cream
1   tablespoon butter   1/2 cup lavender flowers

In a heavy saucepan or skillet, melt the butter and stir in the flour. When completely blended and quite thick, gradually add the cream, stirring constantly. When the sauce becomes thick, add the flowers, remove from the heat and serve over baked chicken breasts or pork roast. Makes enough sauce for 2 servings.

LAVENDER SORBET

This takes two days, so plan ahead.

5 cups bottled drinking water	1/2 cup blush wine
2 cups sugar	5 tablespoons fresh orange juice
1/3 cup lavender flowers	6 lavender flower heads for garnish

Put the first three ingredients in a heavy pan. Bring to a boil, stirring to increase the temperature and dissolve the sugar more quickly. When the syrup starts to boil, reduce the heat and simmer for five minutes. Let cool and refrigerate at least eight hours—overnight is preferable. Add the wine and juice. Pour into a freezer container and store in freezer. Every hour, stir the mix to break up the ice, giving the sorbet a smoother consistency. It will be ready to serve after 8 - 10 hours. You can use an electric ice cream machine to freeze the sorbet. Makes 6 servings.

LAVENDER MERINGUES

2 egg whites, room temperature	4 tablespoons lavender flowers
1/2 teaspoon cream of tartar	12 fresh sprigs of lavender flower
7 tablespoons sugar	heads, optional

In a glass bowl, beat the egg whites and cream of tartar until stiff. Begin adding the sugar one tablespoon at a time, making sure that the sugar is completely absorbed before adding the next tablespoon. When meringue becomes shiny and the peaks very firm, add the lavender flowers. Place wax paper over a cookie sheet. Using a large spoon, drop 12 - 15 dollops of meringue on the cookie sheet. Place in a pre-warmed oven of 250°F and bake for 50 minutes. Remove the meringues very carefully with a spatula. These can be served by themselves or floated in a sauce or filled with ice cream or fruit. Garnish with more lavender flower heads.

From Executive Chef Paul Brenholt,
Deep Ellum Cafe, Inc., Dallas, Texas

MARJORAM
The heady fragrance and soft downy leaves makes this herb a must in your garden. Marjoram is used as one of the main ingredients in bouquet garnis and roasts of all kinds. Marjoram leaves are used in stuffings, salads, eggs, cheese, soups, stews, salad dressings, puddings, muffins, pies and cakes. Dried leaves are rubbed over lamb, veal, pork and poultry. A paste similar to that suggested for basil will preserve fresh marjoram for one year. For drying instructions, refer to the Cultivation chapter.

CLASSIC BOUQUET GARNIS

6   sprigs of marjoram—4 to 6 inches   2   sprigs of thyme—same
    long   2   sprigs of sage—same
4   sprigs of rosemary—same

Tie all of the herbs together with a string and insert into the cavity of any bird weighing up to 10 pounds. Truss and bake as normal. Remove the herbs before carving and use as a garnish on the platter. Or the garnis may be added to stews about 15 minutes before serving. Remove and discard.

MARJORAM GRAVY

3   tablespoons butter   1/2 cup red wine
3   tablespoons flour   Sea salt and black pepper to taste
2   cups of stock (chicken, beef or 3   tablespoons fresh marjoram
    vegetable)

In a heavy skillet, melt the butter and gradually add the flour, stir until a smooth paste. Next gradually add the stock, stirring after each 1/4 cup has been added, blending completely. When all of the stock has been added and the gravy is smooth and thick, add the wine, sea salt and black pepper to taste. Continue to stir and cook until the gravy has again reached the desired consistency. Add the marjoram, stir to blend and serve. Makes 3 cups of gravy. Good over baked potatoes or rice as well as roasts and chicken.

SEVICHE STYLE CALAMARI AND SHRIMP SALAD WITH MARJORAM

1   pound cleaned squid cut into
    rounds, include tentacles
1   pound cleaned and deveined
    medium shrimp
1/2 cup fresh lemon juice

1   cup basil vinegar
1/2 cup tarragon or olive oil
2   cloves of garlic, minced
1/2 cup chopped scallions
2   tablespoons minced marjoram

In a heavy skillet, cook the squid and shrimp in the lemon juice until pink. Drain all but 3 tablespoons of the liquid and place shrimp mixture in a large mixing bowl. In a small mixing bowl, add the next 5 ingredients and blend thoroughly, using a whisk. Toss the shrimp and scallions with the oil and vinegar dressing and chill in the refrigerator for 6 hours. Serve with lemon wedges and sea salt. Makes 4 large servings.

HEARTY BLACK BEAN AND RICE SOUP WITH MARJORAM

1   pound of black beans cooked
    according to package instructions
4   cloves of garlic, minced
2   bay leaves
1   cup diced onions

1   16 ounce can of stewed tomatoes
2   cups cooked rice
1   cup red wine
1   teaspoon thyme
3   teaspoons marjoram

In a large heavy pan, add beans — drained — to next 4 ingredients. Add water to cover. Bring to a boil and simmer for 1 hour. Add rice and wine, continuing to simmer for another 45 minutes. Add thyme and marjoram and any salt or pepper to taste. Stir to blend. Ham or cooked sausage can be added with the rice and wine. Serves 8 - 10.

CARROT AND MARJORAM MUFFINS

1 1/4 cups unbleached flour
1/2 teaspoon baking soda
1 teaspoon double-acting baking
    powder
1/2 teaspoon salt

2 tablespoons butter
1 egg
1/3 cup buttermilk
1 cup shredded carrots
1/4 cup minced marjoram

In a small mixing bowl, combine the first 4 ingredients. In a large mixing bowl, cream together the next 3 ingredients until smooth and golden, add the carrots and marjoram and blend well. Stir in the flour mixture until moist. Place a spoonful of batter in muffin tins and cook in a preheated 400°F oven for 15 minutes — check with a tester. Makes 12 muffins.

MINT

There are so many varieties of mint that the total number may never be known. Hot or cold, mint tea is hard to duplicate for its aroma and taste any time of year. Mint oils and vinegars when used by themselves or blended with other herbs are a welcome addition to marinades and sauces. Mint may be dried in a 200°F oven for about 30 minutes, or until very brittle. Store in an airtight jar in the icebox. Will keep for 4 months. My favorites include peppermint, spearmint, bergamont, applemint and lemon mint.

SPEARMINT brings out the flavors of other ingredients and adds a "cool" taste. Use it in relishes, fruit salads, jellies, jams, sauces for lamb and veal, summer vegetables such as new peas, beans and carrots, as a garnish for desserts and as a decorative and flavorful addition to icings and puddings of all kinds.

BERGAMONT has a citrus taste and aroma. It lends itself to poultry, pork, salads and desserts. A stronger flavor and aroma than other mints, bergamont should be used sparingly. Many chefs like the larger leaf and reddish complexion of this mint and use it often as a garnish.

APPLEMINT has a new green look, a downy feel and a wonderful apple aroma. A great dessert mint welcomed in muffins, breads, pies, puddings and fruit salads, as well as sauces and stuffings for pork, poultry and game.

LEMON MINT looks like a lighter colored spearmint. When you brush against it or cut it, the aroma of fresh squeezed lemons is pungent and refreshing. Goes well with seafood of all kinds or in sauces for broccoli and cauliflower. In fruit salads, cookies, puddings, pound cakes and pies, and in tea, this delightful mint has an important place in my recipe file.

PEPPERMINT is mostly used for medicinal purposes due to the quantity of menthol in its chemical structure. Peppermint promotes the appetite and acts as a breath freshener. Because of its bold taste, peppermint should be used conservatively, substituting 1/2 of the measurement for other mints.

MINT AND FRUIT SALAD

1 cup diced or balled honeydew melon	1 cup diced mango
1 cup diced strawberries	1/4 cup of spearmint or lemon mint leaves, minced
1 cup mixed green and red seedless grapes	1/2 large lemon or lime
	8 mint sprigs

In a large glass bowl, gently stir the fruit with a wooden spoon. Add the mint and juice from the lemon or lime and toss 30 times. Garnish with additional whole mint leaves. Makes 8 servings.

FRESH PEPPERMINT ICE CREAM

1/4 pound fresh peppermint	5 eggs
2 quarts whipping cream	1/8 teaspoon salt
2 1/2 cups sugar	1 tablespoon clear vanilla extract
3 cups half and half	1 tablespoon peppermint extract

There is no need to de-stem the peppermint, just thoroughly wash and rinse. Place sugar, peppermint and cream in a double boiler. Cover and let them slowly steep until the mint has lost its color and the cream gets a subtle green tint. Pour cream mix through a fine mesh strainer and mash the mint with back of a spoon until all the liquid is forced through the strainer. Return the cream base back to the double boiler.

In a mixing bowl, thoroughly beat the eggs and half and half together. Whip the cream base as you gradually pour this mix in. Heat until 165°F. Remove cream mix from heat and cool.

Next, add salt and extracts. Refrigerate overnight and freeze the next day in an ice cream freezer. Should make 3/4 to one gallon of ice cream.

Variation: Try using same amount of fresh lavender or rosemary extract for a different twist.

From Scotty Griffey, the Executive Chef at Flip's Wine Bar, Dallas, Texas

❖ Add 4 teaspoons of lemon mint to your favorite pound cake.

31

SUMMER VEGETABLES WITH MINT

3   tablespoons sesame or olive oil
2   yellow squash or 1 large zucchini
1   cup snow peas, ends removed

1   carrot, finely diced
2   tablespoons fresh spearmint or
    applemint, minced

In a large, heavy skillet, heat the oil. When the oil is very hot, stir in the vegetables. Continue to stir for two minutes. Remove from the heat and add the fresh mint, stirring until well blended. Serves 4 as a side dish.

SPICED SUMMER TEA

6   cups water
1/2 cup bergamont mint
1/2 cup lemon mint
6   teaspoons sugar

1   cup orange juice
6   sprigs of bergamont mint
6   sprigs of lemon mint

Boil water in saucepan. Put next 3 ingredients in boiling water and remove the pan from the stove. Let steep, covered, for 20 minutes. Add the orange juice, pour into glasses, add ice and mint sprigs. Makes 6 glasses.

MINT SAUCE

2   teaspoons sugar
1/3 cup spearmint or 1/4 cup
    applemint, minced fine

1/2 cup water
2   tablespoons vinegar
1   tablespoon lemon juice

In a saucepan, combine sugar and mint until well blended, add the next 3 ingredients, bring to a fast boil. Remove from heat and let cool. Strain. Serve with lamb, pork or use as the vinegar portion in a salad dressing.

❖ In your favorite shrimp or chicken salad, add 1 teaspoon of fresh lemon mint per cup of salad.

❖ Add 1 teaspoon of bergamont mint per cup of warm chocolate sauce.

❖ When making vanilla ice cream, add 1 teaspoon spearmint or 1/2 teaspoon peppermint to 1 cup of cream.

❖ Add 1 teaspoon applemint or spearmint per cup of fruit to any pie or cobbler.

MINT AND STRAWBERRY MERINGUE CAKE

A delicious, impressive summer dessert.

3 meringue pie shells *
3 pints ripe strawberries — sliced thin (reserve 1 pint for top)
1 pint whipping cream

10 tablespoons sugar
1/2 cup minced spearmint leaves
20 mint leaves for garnish

Whip cream, adding 1 tablespoon sugar at a time until completely dissolved. When cream is thick, add mint leaves blending thoroughly. Place one meringue shell on the serving dish, layer with 1/3 of the whipping cream mixture and 1/2 of the sliced strawberries. Add the next meringue shell, layering 1/3 of the cream and the remaining sliced strawberries. Top with the last shell, layer with remaining cream. Halve the remaining strawberries and arrange on the top in circles, placing mint leaves in between circles and on outside of layers. Chill for at least 6 hours before serving. Serves 10 - 12.

* Meringue Shells — can be made a day in advance.
6 large egg whites — room temperature
1/2 teaspoon salt

1/2 teaspoon cream of tartar
1/2 cup sugar
3/4 teaspoon vanilla

Combine first 3 ingredients in a glass or ceramic bowl. Beat on high speed until soft peaks form. Beat in the sugar one tablespoon at a time until very stiff peaks form; add vanilla. (The egg whites must be very stiff but moist.) Make 3 9-inch circles on brown or wax paper. Spread meringue mixture 1/4-inch thick on each circle. Place on cookie sheets and bake in a 250°F oven for 1 hour. Turn off the oven and let the meringues cool gradually in the oven for 30 minutes to an hour. Remove meringues from paper carefully and store in the ice box until ready to layer.

OREGANO is most associated with Italian, Greek and South and Central American dishes. Soups, stews, egg, cheese, salad dressings, oil and vinegars, risottos and pasta dishes all benefit from the addition of fresh oregano. Dried, it can be rubbed on beef, chicken and fish. It is one of the most versatile herbs in your garden. Enjoy experimenting with different varieties. These recipes use upright or the creeping Greek varieties.

OREGANO FRIED CHEESE

12 ounces provolone or mozzarella
    cheese, cut into 1-inch cubes
1/4 cup cornstarch
1 egg, beaten
1 cup bread crumbs, finely crushed

1/2 teaspoon garlic powder
1 teaspoon fresh oregano, minced, or
    1/2 teaspoon dried oregano
    Oil for frying

Mix the bread crumbs, garlic and oregano together. Coat the cheese cubes with the cornstarch doing several cubes at a time then dip into the egg, coating thoroughly. Coat the cubes with the bread crumb mixture and fry in very hot oil for no more than 2 minutes. Use a slotted spoon to remove the cubes from the oil and drain well on paper towels. Transfer to a warm oven while frying the rest. Serve with ranch or marinara sauce and lemon wedges. Makes 24 cubes.

HERBED WILD RICE

1 tablespoon olive oil
1 cup wild rice, rinsed and drained
2 cups chicken or vegetable broth
1 minced garlic clove

2 tablespoons fresh minced oregano
1 teaspoon fresh thyme
1 tablespoon lemon juice
    Sea salt and black pepper to taste

Place the oil and rice in a heavy pan and cook over moderate heat for 2-3 minutes, stirring constantly. Add the broth and garlic, bring to a boil. Reduce heat and simmer for approximately 1 hour or until all liquid has been absorbed. Stir in the last 4 ingredients and cook an additional 5 minutes. Serve hot or cold. Makes 6 servings.

OREGANO RATATOUILLE

5   tablespoons olive oil
1   large eggplant, peeled and diced
2   zucchini, diced
1/2 cup onion, diced
2   8-ounce cans of Italian stewed
    tomatoes
3   cloves of garlic, minced

Sea salt and black pepper to taste
1   teaspoon Worcestershire sauce
1/2 teaspoon sugar
2   tablespoons fresh minced oregano
1/2 tablespoon fresh minced thyme
2   tablespoons fresh basil leaves,
    minced

In a heavy skillet, heat the olive oil, add the next 3 ingredients, stir until completely coated with the oil. Cook over moderate heat for 8-10 minutes, stirring frequently. Add the next 5 ingredients, stirring to blend thoroughly. Cover and simmer for 15 minutes, stirring frequently. Add the last 3 ingredients and cook for an additional 3-5 minutes. Serve with faccacio or garlic bread and salad. Serves 4.

MARINATED CHICKEN BREASTS WITH OREGANO

1/2 cup lemon or lime juice
1/4 cup white wine vinegar
2   tablespoons fresh minced oregano
1   tablespoon fresh thyme

1   tablespoon fresh minced basil
3   minced garlic cloves
    Sea salt and white pepper to taste
4   chicken breasts, skin removed

Combine the first 7 ingredients. Pour into a shallow pan large enough to accommodate the chicken breasts lying in one layer. Cover the chicken with the marinade, turning the chicken to coat both sides. Cover the pan and refrigerate for at least 8 hours or overnight. Drain the marinade, reserving for basting. Broil for approximately 15 minutes, turning and basting every 4-5 minutes. Prick the chicken with a fork and if clear liquid runs out, the chicken is done. Serve hot or cold. Makes 4 servings.

OREGANO OYSTER DRESSING

1   pound oysters and liquid
1   cup water
1/2 cup butter—2 sticks
1   cup onion, diced fine
1   cup celery, diced fine with strings
    removed
1   teaspoon garlic powder
1   teaspoon paprika

1 1/2   tablespoons minced fresh
        oregano
1   tablespoon fresh minced thyme
    Sea salt and black pepper to taste
2   bay leaves
1 1/2   cups dry bread crumbs,
        crushed fine
1/2 cup chopped green onions

Pour oysters and their liquid into a bowl, add the water and refrigerate for about 1 hour. Pour off the liquid and save. In a heavy skillet, melt the butter and sauté the onion and celery, cooking until the onion is clear. Meanwhile, mix the next 5 ingredients together and add 1/4 to the skillet, blending thoroughly. Cook for two minutes. Stir in the oyster water, cooking over high heat until reduced by 1/4. Add the bread crumbs, and the rest of the oregano mixture. Stir until moistened. Remove from heat and stir in the oysters and bay leaves. Transfer the dressing to an ungreased baking pan and cook uncovered for 30-40 minutes at 350°F. Discard bay leaves before serving. Makes 3 - 4 cups of dressing.

❖ In your favorite hot potato salad, add 1 teaspoon fresh oregano per cup of salad. Mix and serve.

❖ Add 1 tablespoon oregano to every cup of batter for fried foods.

❖ Rub dried oregano over whole fish before grilling or broiling.

❖ Add 1 teaspoon of fresh oregano to 1 cup of gazpacho, salsa or hot sauce.

PARSLEY

One of the most abused and misunderstood herbs in the garden. Seen primarily as a garnish, it is often discarded when the plates are cleared. This plant is loaded with vitamins A, E, and C, and minerals like iron, calcium and phosphates and is an extremely versatile herb due to its subtle taste. There are several kinds of parsley all with their unique appearance, taste and use. Curly parsley is the most recognized and is used for culinary and medicinal purposes. Italian or flat leaf parsley has a much longer stalk and is mostly used as a culinary herb. Hamburg parsley is grown for its root and is used much as a parsnip. Chervil has very lacy leaves and a delicate anise or tarragon taste which gives it a special advantage. French chefs prefer chervil in the kitchen over most other varieties. Parsley can be used in all but dessert dishes. It enhances the taste of other ingredients and adds color and aroma to any dish. It may be frozen and used in that form for soups and stews, etc. If used fresh, always add during the last five minutes. Keep using it as a garnish, but for your sake put it in your stomach, too!

FRIED PARSLEY

1   *bunch Italian or curly parsley*   *Parmesan cheese, finely grated*
     Oil for frying

In a skillet, heat the oil until almost smoking. Drop in the parsley, a little at a time. When it turns a bright green, take out with a slotted spoon and drain on paper towels. Sprinkle with Parmesan cheese and serve at once. This makes a great hors d'oeuvres or side dish.

❖ Parsley can be added to any entrée. Always remember to add it just before serving. Remember that the chervil variety will add a slight tarragon flavor.

❖ In salads, add 2 tablespoons per cup of salad.

CHERVIL CREAM SAUCE

1   cup cream
6   tablespoons chervil
3   tablespoons butter
1 1/2   tablespoons flour

1 1/2   cups stock—chicken or
      vegetable
1   clove garlic, minced
      Sea salt and white pepper

In a heavy saucepan, heat the cream, then add the chervil. Remove from the heat and let stand for 15-20 minutes. In a skillet, melt the butter, add the garlic and gradually add the flour, stirring all the time to insure a smooth paste. Gradually add the stock, stir to keep the sauce smooth and thick. Add the cream mixture and sea salt and pepper to taste. Serve over boiled new potatoes, oven baked chicken, rice or baked fish. Makes approximately 1 cup of sauce.

PARSLEY SPAGHETTI

1/2 pound spaghetti, cooked al dente
1/3 cup melted butter
1/2 cup fresh Italian parsley, minced

3/4 cup fresh Parmesan cheese, grated
Ground black pepper

Combine the last 4 ingredients, blending well. Toss with the spaghetti and serve very warm. Grind plenty of fresh black pepper over each serving. Makes 2 servings.

PARSLEY POTATOES IN JACKETS

8   small new potatoes, washed and
      dried
4   teaspoons butter, melted
8   teaspoons minced fresh parsley—
      Italian or chervil

1 1/2   teaspoons sea salt
2   teaspoons black pepper

In a bowl, mix the parsley, salt and pepper. Roll the new potatoes in the melted butter and then in the parsley mix. Wrap potatoes in foil and bake at 350°F in a shallow pan for 30 minutes or until the potatoes are done. Serves 3 - 4.

EGGPLANT WITH PARSLEY

1	*pound eggplant, peeled and diced*
1	*cup diced onion*
3	*tablespoons oil*
1/2 cup fresh minced Italian parsley	

1/3 cup freshly grated Parmesan cheese
1/2 cup finely crushed dry bread crumbs

In a heavy skillet, heat the oil and cook the onion until transparent. Add the eggplant and cook an additional 10 minutes, stirring often. Remove from the stove and stir in 1/3 cup of the parsley. Transfer to a shallow pan. Combine the Parmesan cheese, bread crumbs and remaining parsley, sprinkle over the top of the eggplant mixture and cook uncovered for approximately 30-45 minutes at 350°F. Serves 2.

PARSLEY, SAGE, ROSEMARY AND THYME VINEGAR

1   *16-ounce amber colored jar*
1/2 *pound Italian parsley*
1/4 *pound sage*

1/4 *pound rosemary*
1/4 *pound thyme*
2   *cups white vinegar*

Stuff all ingredients into the amber jar, macerating every 1/4 of the way to bruise the herbs. Pour in the vinegar, screw lid on tightly and set in a warm, sunny window. Turn the jar over every day for 2 - 3 weeks. Decant into clear bottles and add a fresh sprig of each of the herbs. This makes an excellent marinade for poultry, fish, pork and vegetables as well as dressing for salads.

❖ Add 1 tablespoon minced parsley per cup of soup, sauce or stew. Each variety of parsley will impart a slightly different taste.

ROSEMARY is a truly noble herb and is the herb of remembrance and friendship. Looking like a small Christmas tree and smelling of pine and cloves, rosemary is a joy not only in the kitchen but also throughout the whole house. Rosemary is used with poultry, lamb, fish, shellfish, pork, game, nuts, cream cheeses, casseroles, rice, pasta, vegetable dishes, muffins, steamed puddings, breads, and as an oil or vinegar in salads and marinades. The long branches can be used as an aromatic and flavorful skewer for shish-ke-bob. To store rosemary for future use, place in a 200°F to 250°F oven for approximately one hour. As soon as the rosemary is crisp to the touch, let cool and immediately crumble and store in an airtight jar, keeping it out of direct light. Or you can place the fresh rosemary leaves in a blender with just enough oil to make a paste. Spoon the paste into an airtight jar and store in the refrigerator. This will keep fresh for 6 - 9 months.

ROASTED WALNUTS WITH ROSEMARY

1   *pound walnut halves*
4   *tablespoons fresh rosemary*
1/2 *stick butter*

2   *tablespoons garlic salt*
6   *fresh rosemary sprigs for garnish*

In a saucepan, melt the butter, add the rosemary and garlic salt and remove from stove. Add the walnuts and stir until completely coated. Place the walnuts on a cookie sheet and roast in a 200°F oven for 30 - 45 minutes. Serve warm with fresh rosemary sprigs as garnish. This is an especially good dish served in the fall and winter months.

❖ Add 1 teaspoon of crushed rosemary to 1 cup of muffin mix. These are delicious!

❖ Add 1/3 cup of crushed rosemary leaves to 8-inch pizza just before serving.

ROSEMARY ITALIAN PASTA

1 pound rigatoni, cooked al dente
4 tablespoons olive oil
1/2 cup onion, diced small
6 sundried tomatoes, softened in hot oil, drained and chopped fine
2 garlic cloves, minced
2 tablespoons fresh rosemary leaves, minced

1 tablespoon fresh oregano leaves, minced
2 tablespoons fresh Italian parsley
1/2 cup Calamata olives, seeded and chopped fine
1/3 cup Asiago or Romano cheese, freshly grated

In a heavy skillet, heat the oil, add the onion and cook until transparent. Stir in the next 6 ingredients. Pour mixture over the pasta and toss. Sprinkle the cheese over each serving. Serves 4.

ROSEMARY KE-BOBS

4 16-inch rosemary branches, leaves removed except for last 3 inches
1 1/2 pounds of lamb roast, cut into 2-inch cubes and marinated*
3 sweet onions, quartered
4 ripe tomatoes, cut in half then wedged

2 green peppers, cut in 2-inch pieces
1 golden pepper, cut in 2-inch pieces
8 cloves of garlic, split
Sea salt and pepper to taste

Marinade:
1/2 cup olive or rosemary oil
3/4 cup red wine vinegar
2 cloves garlic

1/4 cup lemon juice
Sea salt and pepper

Combine all ingredients for marinade and pour over lamb. Refrigerate overnight.

On the rosemary skewers, begin with a strip of yellow pepper followed by onion, tomato, meat, garlic, meat, green pepper, onion, etc., until full. Grill 5 inches away from heat, turning frequently and basting with the marinade until done, approximately 20 minutes. Serve with rice and salad. Serves 4.

WHOLE BAKED FISH WITH ROSEMARY

4   *whole fillets, gutted and cleaned*
8   *sprigs of rosemary, 4 inches long*
4   *sprigs of thyme, 4 inches long*
1   *stick of butter*
1/3 *cup of lemon juice*

2   *garlic cloves, minced*
1   *shallot, diced*
4   *tablespoons minced fresh rosemary*
    Sea salt to taste

Place the fish in a shallow pan that has been lined with aluminum foil. Place 2 sprigs of rosemary and 1 sprig of thyme into each fish. In a saucepan, melt the butter adding the next 3 ingredients. Cook for five minutes and pour the sauce over the fish. Cover with aluminum foil and bake at 350°F for 30 minutes or until fish is flaky (use a fork to determine). Baste with sauce and serve. Makes 4 servings.

GRILLED LAMB CHOPS

8   *lamb chops, 1 inch thick*
1/4 *cup olive oil*
1   *teaspoon minced garlic*

2   *tablespoons rosemary*
    Sea salt and black pepper to taste

In a heavy skillet, heat oil and add garlic. As soon as oil is hot, add the lamb chops and sear each side. Reduce heat and cook 10 minutes on each side. Add the rosemary, salt and pepper and serve with mint jelly. Serves 4.

ROSEMARY OIL

1   *8-ounce amber jar*
    Fresh rosemary

1   *cup olive oil*

In an 8-ounce amber jar, stuff as much fresh rosemary as possible into the jar. Macerate to release more of the essential oils. Fill with good olive oil and set in a sunny window. Turn the jar over every day for two weeks. Decant oil into a clear bottle with several fresh sprigs of rosemary. Keep in a cool, dark place. Use as a marinade for all meats and poultry, salad dressings, and in cooked vegetables.

CORNISH HENS
WITH ROSEMARY MUSTARD SAUCE

2   Cornish hens
3   tablespoons olive or rosemary oil
2   tablespoons Dijon mustard,
     country style
1   tablespoon minced fresh rosemary

1/2 tablespoon minced garlic
2   tablespoons lemon juice
     Sea salt and black pepper to taste
4   rosemary sprigs

Rub the hens with oil and place on a roasting rack. Mix together the next 5 ingredients in a bowl, whisking until well blended. Brush the sauce over the hens and place 2 sprigs of rosemary into each cavity. Place in a 400°F oven for 10 minutes, then reduce heat to 350°F. Continue to baste the hens every 10 minutes for 40 minutes or until done. Serves 2 - 4.

MARINATED CORNISH HENS IN HERBS

2   Cornish hens
1/2 cup lemon juice
1/2 cup wine vinegar
1/2 cup olive oil
4   minced garlic cloves
3   tablespoons minced rosemary

2   tablespoons minced oregano
1   tablespoon minced thyme
2   tablespoons minced Italian parsley
1/2 teaspoon onion juice
     Sea salt and pepper to taste

Halve the hens and lay flat in a pan. Whisk together the rest of the ingredients and pour over the hens, turning them to coat completely. Refrigerate overnight. Grill or broil the hens for approximately 20 minutes, basting often with the marinade. Serves 4.

❖ Add 1/4 cup crushed rosemary leaves to 8 ounces Philadelphia cream cheese. Let sit at room temperature for 1 hour or four hours in refrigerator. Use as a spread or serve over baked whole new potatoes.

SAGE
A wise person once said that as long as there was sage in your garden you should never be sick or die. Mostly associated with dressing and onion dishes, sage is an excellent addition to fish, game, lamb, pasta, sauces, soups, stews, rice, pork, cheese, jellies, cream cheese and beans. The larger leaves can be dusted with a light batter and fried and served as a separate dish or as a garnish with meat. The blue and pink flowers are a beautiful garnish or can be substituted for the leaves in most recipes. Sage may be stored dried or as a paste — see *Rosemary* and follow the same instructions.

SAGE MAYONNAISE

2	large egg yolks	1	tablespoon minced fresh sage
2	teaspoons wine vinegar	1	tablespoon lemon juice
1	teaspoon country-style Dijon mustard		Sea salt to taste
		1 1/4	cups vegetable oil

Mix the first 6 ingredients in a blender. Very slowly add the oil, emulsifying completely. Store in an airtight container in the refrigerator. Especially good in chicken salads, with hot or cold pork and most sandwiches.

SAGE FRITTERS

24	sage leaves—the large golden variety	1/2	cup unbleached flour
1	tablespoon butter	1/3	cup milk
1/3	cup water	1	egg
			Oil for frying

Wash the sage leaves and blot dry with paper towels. In a saucepan, melt the butter in the water. Mix the next 3 ingredients and add the butter-water, stirring until batter is smooth and thick. Heat the oil in a skillet until almost smoking. Dip the sage leaves in the batter and fry a few at a time, turning to fry both sides evenly. Drain on paper towels, transferring to a pre-warmed oven until all are done. Serve at once.

SAGE PORK ROAST

1	4-pound tenderloin of pork	2	tablespoons fresh thyme
4	tablespoons fresh dried sage, crushed	2	tablespoons garlic salt
		2	tablespoons black pepper

Combine last 4 ingredients and roll the pork tenderloin in them until completely covered. Place on a roasting rack and set in a 400°F oven for 10 minutes, reducing the heat to 350°F and cook 25 minutes per pound. Continue to baste every 10 minutes with the drippings in the pan. Let stand for 10 minutes out of the oven before slicing.

CARROTS IN SAGE/GINGER SAUCE

1	pound early or small carrots, washed and trimmed	1	tablespoon brown sugar
		1	tablespoon fresh minced ginger
1/2 stick butter		2	tablespoons fresh minced sage

In a heavy saucepan, place the carrots with 1/2 inch water and bring to a boil. Reduce heat and simmer for 10 minutes. Using a wooden spoon, stir in the next 4 ingredients, and cook for another 3-5 minutes. Serve in the juice. Even better the next day. Serves 4.

PINEAPPLE SAGE TEA

2	cups water	3	tablespoons pineapple sage leaves
2	bags of regular tea	2	pineapple sage sprigs for glasses
2	tablespoons honey		

Steep bags in boiling water for 5 minutes. Remove from heat and add honey and pineapple sage. Let steep for 15 minutes. Strain and pour into glasses. Add ice and pineapple sage sprigs and serve. Makes 2 glasses.

OVEN BAKED FRIED CHICKEN

4	skinned and boned chicken breasts or 8 thighs	1	teaspoon pepper
1	stick of butter	1	tablespoon minced garlic
1	cup flour	2	tablespoons minced sage
1	teaspoon sea salt	1	tablespoon minced oregano

Melt butter in a roasting pan that is large enough to accomodate the chicken in a single layer. Combine next 6 ingredients in a plastic bag, shaking well to blend. Put several pieces of chicken in the bag and shake to coat evenly. Arrange chicken in the pan and bake at 350°F for 30 minutes, turn chicken and cook an additional 25 minutes. Very succulent with a nice crispy texture. Serves 4.

SAGE ONION RINGS

2	large Bermuda onions — cut 1/2-inch thick	2	tablespoons minced sage
1	cup flour	1	large egg — beaten
1/2 teaspoon sea salt		2/3	cup water or beer

Blend first 3 ingredients together, add egg and water (or beer) to make a smooth paste. Dip onion rings in batter and fry several at a time in very hot vegetable oil. They are done when they rise to the top of the oil. Remove from oil with a slotted spoon, place on paper towels, and keep warm until all onion rings are fried.

❖ 1/4 cup of fresh sage leaves, minced, to 1 8-ounce package cream cheese. Let stand at room temperature for 1 hour or refrigerate for 4 hours. Serve with bagel chips or toast points. Very refreshing especially in the summer.

❖ Put 1 tablespoon minced sage leaves to 1 cup of meat or poultry stuffing.

❖ Add 1/2 tablespoon fresh minced sage leaves over 1 pound pâté.

SORREL is a harbinger of spring. Sending out its small arrow

shaped leaves and tangy lemony fragrance, filling every garden with hope and promise that winter's bleakness is ending. Sorrel is a delightfully refreshing addition to salads, sandwiches, sauces for seafood and chicken, egg dishes, beans, soups and vegetables. Every garden should include this beautiful and beneficial plant.

SORREL STUFFED WITH GOAT CHEESE AND PIMENTO

Take a large slice of pimento (fresh would be nice but they are extremely difficult to find). Surround it with goat cheese. I prefer fresh Texas Goat from the Mozzarella Company in Dallas, Texas or Montrachet — a French goat cheese. Place on a sorrel leaf and roll it up. Lightly drizzle with your favorite dressing before serving. The sundried tomato vinaigrette works extremely well on this dish. Serve as an appetizer, preferably at room temperature.

SUNDRIED TOMATA VINAIGRETTE

18-20 *pieces sundried tomatoes,*
     soak for 10 minutes and rinse
     (2 ounces — do not buy the ones
     in olive oil)
1   *ounce fresh basil, washed and*
     de-stemmed

1/2 *cup balsamic vinegar*
     (amount will vary according
     to the quality and type used,
     the better types require less)
1 1/2 *cups extra-virgin olive oil*

Place sundried tomatoes, fresh basil and balsamic vinegar in a food processor and puree. Gradually add olive oil and puree till liquefied. A little shallot works well in this vinaigrette. The extra-virgin might be too strong for some people, so you might want to cut back to half olive and half vegetable oil. A little goes a long way with this vinaigrette. Makes a little over 2 cups.

From Scotty Griffey, the Executive Chef at
Flip's Wine Bar, Dallas, Texas

SORREL AND LOX PINWHEELS

1/4 pound of lox or smoked salmon
8 large leaves of sorrel
4 ounces cream cheese, room temperature

1 lemon
3 ounces capers
Fresh cracked pepper

Discard the center stem of the sorrel leaves, leaving two halves per leaf. Place a piece of lox on each leaf. Add a dollop of cream cheese and a few capers. Roll and secure with a toothpick. When all of the lox has been rolled with sorrel leaves, place on a platter and squeeze lemon juice over them. Sprinkle with fresh pepper and cool in the refrigerator for 2-3 hours covered with wax paper. Makes 12 - 16.

A REFRESHING SUMMER SALAD

2 cups of torn sorrel leaves
1 cup of torn Bibb lettuce
1/2 cup of torn arugula leaves

2 tablespoons basil vinegar
4 tablespoons tarragon oil
1 tablespoon lemon juice

Mix the salads together in large wooden salad bowl. Combine the last 3 ingredients and whisk together well. Pour over the salad and toss 30 times. Serve with pepper to taste.

SHRIMP AND SORREL SALAD

1 pound medium shrimp, cooked and deveined
2 tablespoons capers
1/2 cup chopped celery
1/2 large avocado, peeled and diced

1 cup torn sorrel leaves
1 teaspoon minced garlic
1/4 cup lemon juice
1/2 cup mayonnaise

Combine the first 5 ingredients and toss well, using wooden spoons to keep from bruising the avocado. Mix together the last 3 ingredients and add to the shrimp mixture. Toss 30 times. Serve at room temperature or slightly chilled. Serves 3 - 4.

CREAMY SORREL SOUP

2   cups chicken or vegetable broth
2   tablespoons minced onion
1/3 pound sorrel leaves
1   tablespoon minced garlic

1   cup yogurt
1   cup half and half
    Sea salt and black pepper to taste

In a heavy pan bring broth to a boil, add next 3 ingredients and simmer for 10 minutes. Remove from heat, cool slightly and puree in a food processor or blender. Return to stove, add next 2 ingredients, stir until well blended and heated through. Add sea salt and pepper to taste. May be served warm or chilled. A wonderfully refreshing lemony soup for any time of the year. Serves 4.

SORREL AND ALBACORE SANDWICHES

6   sorrel leaves — torn
1   6-ounce can albacore
1   tablespoon lemon juice
1   teaspoon minced garlic

3   tablespoons mayonnaise
1   tablespoon mustard
1   tablespoon caviar — optional

Mix all ingredients together until well blended. Spread on sour dough or whole wheat buns. A very unique and sophisticated taste. Perfect for tailgate or romantic picnics. Makes 2.

❖ Fish fillets can be wrapped or laid on a bed of sorrel and steamed or poached. The fish will have a subtle lemon taste.

❖ Add 1/2 cup of torn sorrel leaves to 2 cups of chicken salad.

❖ Add 1/2 cup of torn sorrel leaves to vegetable or cream soups for a refreshing lemony taste.

❖ Add 1/4 cup of torn sorrel leaves to 1 cup of basic cream sauce. Use with fish, shellfish or chicken dishes.

TARRAGON
Associated with French cuisine, this lovely, slightly licorice tasting herb benefits most sauces, oils and vinegars. Tarragon can be added to eggs, chicken, lamb, fish and shellfish, pickles, artichokes, peas, carrots and herbed butters. Known for its flavoring of vinegar and rémoulade sauce, try marinating lamb, chicken and pork with a combination of tarragon vinegar, lemon and olive oil. This herb is best used fresh. If storage is necessary, then freeze it, as drying very often changes the taste to an inferior product.

TARRAGON VINAIGRETTE

3/4 cup olive oil
1/4 cup tarragon vinegar
2   tablespoons lemon or lime juice
1   clove garlic, minced

4   tablespoons fresh tarragon, minced
Sea salt and ground black pepper
to taste

Whisk together all ingredients but the oil. Add the oil in a drizzle, whisking constantly until completely emulsified. Store in the refrigerator. Can be used as a marinade for chicken, fish or beef fillets. Makes 1 cup.

TARRAGON CREAM OF CHICKEN SOUP

5   cups chicken stock
4   tablespoons minced fresh tarragon
4   tablespoons butter
2   tablespoons flour
2   cups of heavy cream or 1 cup sour
     cream and 1 cup yogurt

2   teaspoons lemon juice
     Sea salt and white pepper to taste
2   breasts of chicken, baked or broiled,
     skinned and diced

Heat the chicken stock for 5 minutes. Add the tarragon leaves, remove from heat and let stand for 15-20 minutes. In a heavy saucepan, melt the butter and stir in the flour. When a thick paste, gradually add in the cream, stirring constantly. Next add the chicken stock, stirring until blended. Add the lemon juice, salt and pepper and chicken. Heat through and serve. Serves 4.

HOLLANDAISE SAUCE

3   egg yolks
1/2 cup butter
1   tablespoon lemon juice

2   tablespoons minced tarragon
     Sea salt to taste

In a heavy saucepan over moderate heat, stir the egg yolks with the butter until very thick — do not let butter boil. Quickly add in the lemon juice and sea salt, stirring continuously. Add the tarragon and serve immediately over broccoli, asparagus spears, artichoke hearts, fish fillets or boiled shrimp. Makes 1/2 cup approximately.

TARRAGON AND SHRIMP SALAD

1   pound medium shrimp, cooked,
     shelled and diced
1/2 cup mayonnaise (Hellmann's)
1/4 cup lemon juice
2   tablespoons capers, optional

1   teaspoon minced garlic or garlic
     chives
3   tablespoons minced fresh tarragon
1/4 cup pine nuts
     Sea salt and pepper to taste

Put the shrimp in a large bowl and refrigerate. Mix together the rest of the ingredients, blending very well. Add the sauce to the shrimp. Toss well and serve cold. Serves 4.

SWORDFISH STEAKS WITH TARRAGON BUTTER

4   swordfish steaks
1   stick butter
1/4 cup lemon juice

2   cloves of minced garlic
2   tablespoons minced fresh tarragon
     Sea salt and black pepper to taste

In a skillet, melt the butter, add next 4 ingredients and blend well. Set aside. Grill the steaks for about 4 minutes on each side, or until done. Pour the sauce over and serve at once. Serves 4.

CHICKEN THIGHS WITH TARRAGON SAUCE

8	chicken thighs		3	tablespoons minced tarragon
1	tablespoon butter		1	teaspoon minced garlic chives or
1	tablespoon unbleached flour			garlic
1/2	onion, peeled and finely diced			Sea salt and black pepper to taste
1/2	cup heavy cream		1/2	cup minced parsley — Italian or
1/2	cup chicken stock			chervil
2	tablespoons sherry or port			

In a heavy roasting pan, place the chicken thighs one layer thick. In a heavy saucepan, melt the butter, add the onions and cook until translucent. Add the flour, stirring until very thick. Gradually add the cream and stock, stirring to maintain a thick sauce consistency. Add the next 5 ingredients. Pour sauce over the chicken and bake at 350°F for 30 minutes. Add the minced parsley just before serving and serve with wild rice and fresh green beans. Serves 4.

EGGPLANT TARRAGON

2	tablespoons olive oil	1/2 cup freshly grated Romano,
1/2	cup diced onions	Parmesan or Asiago cheese
1	eggplant, peeled and diced	1/2 cup dried bread crumbs, crushed
2	tablespoons minced tarragon	fine
1	8-ounce can of stewed tomatoes	

Cook the onion in the olive oil until onion is translucent. Mix in the next 3 ingredients and pour into a baking pan. Combine the last 2 ingredients and sprinkle over the eggplant mixture. Place in a 350°F oven for 40-50 minutes or until eggplant is tender. Serves 2.

❖ Tarragon vinegar is made the same as basil vinegar. Use as a marinade for chicken and fish as well as in salad dressings.

❖ Add 1 tablespoon of minced tarragon to 1 cup tartar sauce for an easy rémoulade-like taste. Serve with shellfish.

THYME
There are hundreds of varieties of thyme, each having different fragrances and tastes. English thyme and lemon thyme are the only ones used in this book. Thyme is wonderful in chowder, lamb, Cajun dishes, veal, poultry, fish, stuffings, sauces, sausages, soups, stews, pastas, rice, eggs, cheese, cream cheese, in oils and vinegars over salads and as marinades, and in bouquet garnis. Steeped in a good white wine for two weeks, the wine becomes a great tonic or before dinner wine. Thyme can be used as a salt substitute. Lemon thyme is wonderful with fish, shellfish, fruit salads, vegetables, breads and muffins. Many a chef has saved a meal by adding thyme, giving bland foods flavor, softening overly seasoned dishes, and giving balance to disharmonious ingredients. You can't go wrong when you add thyme to most any recipe.

ROASTED GARLIC

4   whole heads of garlic   1/2 cup extra-virgin olive oil
4   sprigs fresh thyme

Cut garlic crosswise 3/4-way through—place sprig of fresh thyme in each cut. Place garlic in aluminum foil and drizzle each head with olive oil making sure some gets inside each piece. Wrap foil completely around garlic and bake at 400°F for 1 hour.

From Executive Chef Paul Brenholt,
Deep Ellum Cafe, Inc., Dallas, Texas

THYME AND CHEESE OMELETTE

3   eggs   1/2 cup of soft cheese, Brie, colby,
1   teaspoon thyme   Swiss or cream cheese
1/2 tablespoon chives, minced

Whisk the eggs until very creamy and golden. Pour into an omelette pan. As soon as the edges begin to pucker up, sprinkle the thyme, chives and cheese over 1/2 of the omelette. Fold the other half over, cooking each side to a golden brown. Serve at once with ground pepper.

❖ Use thyme as a substitute for salt in any recipe. A little goes a long way.

CHICKEN AND MUSTARD/THYME SAUCE

1   3-pound chicken, washed and
    patted dry
8   sprigs of fresh thyme
1   cup cream (or plain yogurt)
2   cloves garlic, minced
3   tablespoons fresh thyme or lemon
    thyme

Sea salt and black pepper to taste
2   tablespoons fresh chives, chopped
    fine
1/3 cup country-style mustard
1   teaspoon tarragon wine vinegar

Preheat oven to 400°F. Place chicken in a roasting pan with the fresh sprigs of
thyme in the cavity. Combine the next 8 ingredients, blending thoroughly.
Brush the outside of the chicken with the mustard sauce, putting some in the
cavity. Place the chicken, breast side up, in the oven for 15 minutes. Reduce
heat to 350°F, baste chicken with the sauce every 10 minutes. Cook for an
additional 45 minutes or until the juice runs clear when the chicken is pricked
with a fork. Baste again, remove thyme sprigs form the cavity. Whole new
potatoes and onions can be baked with the chicken. Serves 2 - 4.

BAKED FISH WITH GRAPES AND THYME

8   fillets of white fish, halibut,
    flounder or sole
1/2 cup sour cream
1/2 cup heavy cream
1   cup green seedless grapes, halved

2   teaspoons thyme or lemon thyme
1   teaspoon chives, minced
1/4 cup lemon
Sea salt and white pepper to taste

Preheat oven to 350°F. Place the fillets in a baking dish, one layer thick. Mix
the rest of the ingredients well and pour over the fish. Bake for 30 minutes and
serve with rice pilaf and a salad. Serves 4.

❖ Add 2 tablespoons of thyme to 4 ounces of cream cheese. Blend well and let
   sit for 1 hour at room temperature or 4 hours in the refrigerator. Serve over
   bagels or chips or mix with baked potatoes.

❖ Add 2 teaspoons of lemon thyme to 1 cup of shrimp or chicken salad.

❖ Put 1/3 cup of lemon thyme into a package of prepared stuffing. Cook
   according to directions.

THYME WINE

1   *bottle good white wine*
1 1/2   *cups of English thyme*

1   *24-ounce jar with lid*

Put thyme in the jar, macerating it with a wooden spoon to bruise the leaves. Pour wine over the thyme, secure the lid and place in a cool, dark place for 10 days. Decant the wine into the wine bottle or into a decorative decanter. Four ounces a day will add energy and vitality plus aid the digestion. Especially good for older people.

QUICK AND TASTY CABBAGE

1   *head of cabbage — quartered*
3   *tablespoons rice vinegar or basil vinegar*

2   *tablespoons thyme*
2   *tablespoons sesame seeds*

Put cabbage in a heavy saucepan in 1-2 inches of water. Bring to a boil; cook for 5-6 minutes. Drain. Add next 3 ingredients tossing cabbage lightly to coat. Serve warm with pork, veal or corned beef. Serves 4.

EGGPLANT WITH THYME TOMATO SAUCE

1   *pound eggplant, peeled and sliced*
1/2 *teaspoon sea salt*
1/2 *cup onion, peeled and diced*
1/2 *cup green pepper, diced*
1   *16-ounce can peeled tomatoes — chopped*
1/2 *teaspoon ground pepper*

1   *teaspoon thyme*
1   *tablespoon minced garlic*
1/2 *cup dry bread crumbs — finely crushed*
3/4 *cup shredded Cheddar cheese*
2   *tablespoons minced basil leaves*

Lay eggplant slices in a large pan — no more than 2 layers thick. Sprinkle with sea salt. Combine next 6 ingredients in a bowl and pour over eggplant. Cook in a 400°F oven for 40 minutes. Combine the next 3 ingredients, sprinkle over the top of the eggplant mixture and cook an additional 10 minutes — or until the cheese is melted. Serves 2 for dinner or 4 as a side dish.

Notes:

Cultivation

CULTIVATION INDEX

* For fully cross-referenced index, see page 83.

ARUGULA

An annual, arugula is very easy to grow from seed. It may be sown directly into the garden in a sunny location as soon as the ground can be worked. When the plants are 4" tall, thin to 5". (I cut the roots from these extra tender leaves and use them in salads, soups and sauces.) Leaves that are 6" – 8" long are best. (The longer the leaves, the hotter the taste.) The whole plant can be cut 2" above the ground. Allow 2 weeks before cutting on the same plant. Successive plantings every three weeks will insure a continuous supply. Arugula will self seed if allowed. It can survive a frost but a heavy freeze will kill the roots. Mulching with hay, grass clippings or leaves will help prolong the growing season. Feed the soil around the plants with iron and blood meal or spray with fish emulsion every 3 – 4 weeks. Spray with insecticidal soap and "B.T." for slugs, snails and flea beetles.

BASIL

This annual is extremely susceptible to cold temperatures. The leaves will turn black if temperatures go below 40°F and the whole plant will die at 35°F. In March or early April plant 10 – 15 seeds in a seed flat keeping them moist but not wet and put them in a sunny window. Germination takes 3 – 5 days depending upon the amount of sun available to the seeds. As soon as the first true leaves appear, repot the seedlings into 3" – 4" pots. As soon as the plants are 4" – 6" tall, cut the stem down to the next two true leaves to encourage branching. When these plants are at least 5" tall and the evening temperatures have warmed above 45°F, plant them in a sunny to partial sunny location. Cut as needed but never more than 1/3 of the plant at one time. Always cut just above two nodes, encouraging the plant to bush out. Plant 2 feet apart as some varieties can grow to 4' or more in height. Mulch with leaves, hay or grass clippings 6 inches away from the plant to encourage moist and cool conditions during the summer. Feed a mixture of blood meal, iron and pot ash every three weeks or spray with fish emulsion and sea kelp. Insecticidal soap sprayed every 10 days will discourage worms, caterpillars and slugs. Two weeks before the first frost, cut all the desired leaves you want and pull up the plants. Store the leaves and flowers as suggested in the cooking section. Plants can be transplanted to a greenhouse or overwintered inside. Most herbs do not do well in the house. The humidity and lack of direct sunlight is not conducive to continued growth.

CHIVES

A perennial: I recommend buying starter sets as seeds are very slow and difficult to germinate. Plants can be set out in the early spring or fall in a sunny, well drained location 6 inches apart. Chives like to be kept moist but not wet. Mulch in the summer with leaves, hay or grass clippings. Feed every three weeks with blood meal, iron and bone meal—mixing equal amounts of each—working it into the soil around the roots. Chives need to freeze to insure continued growth next year. Every 3 years divide and plant in a different part of the garden. Chives can be potted up and taken inside to winter over. (Place them in the freezer for 3 days.) Chives are one of the few herbs that will continue to grow inside. Put in a very sunny window and feed once a week.

DILL

An annual: This herb likes full sun and slightly moist conditions. It will grow almost anywhere and seed can be sown directly into the soil. During very hot conditions the seeds do better if shaded. When the plants are 3" tall, thin to 5". Leaves may be cut at any time after the plant is 9" – 12" tall. Do not cut more than 1/2 of the plant. Dill will self seed if allowed. Spray with insecticidal soap every 10 days to prevent infestations of slugs, snails and dill worms. Dill will not grow in the house but can be potted up and taken into the greenhouse. Ducat or baby dill produce the most leaves, mammoth dill produces more seed. Once the seed heads begin to form, the plant will begin to die. If seeds are desired, cut 18" stalks after the seeds have turned a light brown. Hang the cuttings upside down in a dark area. Place a sheet of paper under the dill and collect the seeds as they fall. You can also put bundles of dill cuttings, head first, in paper bags. Hang them up in a closet and shake them gently every day to collect the dill seeds.

LAVENDER

A perennial: Lavender can be grown from seed but is best purchased from a nursery or started from cuttings — soft cuttings in the spring and woody cuttings in the fall. Cuttings should be dipped in hormone solution and then stuck in vermiculite or perlite that is kept very moist for 2 – 3 weeks. The cuttings will have set a good root system and can be transplanted to 4" pots. In approximately 3 weeks the plants will be ready to go to the garden. Lavender likes a light, sandy soil in a sunny location. Leave plenty of room between plants—English lavender can reach a height of 4' – 5' and a diameter of 3' – 4'. There are other varieties such as dwarf lavender that grow to 2' and are good in small gardens or as a container plant. Lavender prefers well drained soil. Dress with compost, well rotted manure or iron and blood meal once a month. The blossoms appear in May and will continue to bloom well into August. Although the flowers have the strongest perfume, the stems and leaves when massed have the same fragrance and can be used year round. If temperatures fall below 25°F, cover with remay cloth or a heavy blanket of hay. Take cuttings in the fall for spring planting just in case your old lavender should die over the winter.

MARIGOLD

An annual: Seeds can be planted directly in the garden from early spring to mid summer. Plant in a sunny location with good drainage. When plants reach 4" – 6" thin to 9", taking those plants that have to be dug up and potting them for additional color on patio, porch or in the house. Cut the flowers back to the next two nodes to increase branching and flowering. A light dressing of compost or manure and phosphate every month will help keep the flowers large and bright. At the end of the growing season cut all of the remaining flowers, bundling them into 10 stalks each and hang them upside down in a dry, dark area. When petals are very brittle, remove and store them in an airtight container away from the light. Use as you would the fresh petals or as a substitute for saffron.

MARJORAM

Marjoram should be considered an annual in all but the warmest climates. Purchase plants or take cuttings. (If cuttings are taken, follow directions for lavender cuttings.) Marjoram belongs to the oregano family and likes full sun, well drained soil and good air circulation. Feed once a month with fish emulsion, sea kelp or a mixture of iron and blood meal. If mildew becomes a problem, spray with zenob and work diatomaceous earth into the soil around the plants. Do not disturb the plants in any way until all signs of mildew are gone. The plants may be cut back by 1/3 to insure continued vigorous growth. In late fall, cut the plants back and dry the stems. When completely dry, rub through a screen that is over a large piece of paper. Collect the dried material into a glass jar, secure tightly and store in a dark area of the pantry. This will stay fresh for 3 – 4 months.

MINT

Perennial: All varieties are grown and cared for much the same way. (There are no seeds for peppermint, so this variety must be grown from cuttings or bought from nursery stock.) Cuttings or divisions in the fall can be planted out in the spring. Cuttings can be rooted in water or potting soil and are ready to plant into the garden in 3 weeks. Mint likes a moist, semi-shaded area that has been fed with a light dressing of bone meal, blood meal and iron. It is advisable to begin new beds every three years as the root system can choke the plants to death. A barrier 10 inches below and 2 inches above the surface around the desired mint bed will prevent the mint from taking over the adjacent garden.

At the end of the summer the plants will begin to get "leggy" looking with bare stalks that are topped with a tuft of leaves and flowers. At this time, cut what leaves are available for winter use. With a weed eater or lawn mower, cut the plants 2" above the ground. If the bed is quite thick, take a shovel and cut the roots every foot or foot and a half to encourage new growth.

If the winters are severe, it is best to cover the bed with a mulch of leaves, hay or remay cloth, or mint may be brought indoors in pots for winter enjoyment. Mint will contract fungus or black leaf if the humidity is high or the ground stays saturated or it is cut or walked on while wet. If this condition begins, spray immediately with zenob and sprinkle diatomaceous earth over the plants. Stay away from the plants until all evidence of this disease is gone. Slugs, snails and flea beetles can be controlled by spraying with insecticidal soap and "B.T." every ten days or as pests are noticed. Note: It is advisable to keep the different varieties of mints separated to avoid cross-pollination.

OREGANO

A perennial: I recommend that you buy plants or take cuttings or divisions. I have had good luck taking cuttings during the new moon of any month from March to September. Place the cuttings in hormone powder and then in vermiculite or perlite that is kept very moist for three weeks. At that time the cuttings will have established a good root system and can be transplanted to 4" pots for another three weeks. These plants can be placed in the garden in a sunny, well drained location, spacing them every 12". A lacing of blood meal and iron or fish emulsion and sea kelp every three weeks will keep the plants healthy during the growing season. Compost can be added in the spring and fall. Oregano needs to be replaced every three years because it becomes too woody to produce fresh leaves. Take cuttings of the most desirable plants and pull up the remainder. Because oregano is subject to mildew and root rot it needs plenty of fresh air circulating around it. Oregano is invasive by nature and a barrier of some kind is recommended. Oregano can survive temperatures into the 20's but will die if temperatures fall into the teen's. Cover with hay, grass clippings or remay cloth to protect the plants during hard freezes. Upright oregano will reach a height of two and one half feet and makes a lovely potted plant. Do not allow upright oregano to flower. Creeping oregano has larger, darker leaves and can be used as a ground cover in shady areas or in hanging baskets. It will grow to nine or twelve inches and will also become very invasive. It produces a beautiful pink to mauve bunch of flowers which are edible and are lovely in oils and vinegars, salads, as dessert garnish, condiments, jams and jellies, or they may be dried for use in floral arrangements, potpourris and wreaths.

PARSLEY

A biennial: Seeds are very difficult to germinate and can take up to five weeks, therefore it is more rewarding to buy the plants. Plant in a cool, moist area that has partial shade. Very hot summers will make the plant mature and flower very quickly. Flowers should be cut to force the plant to produce more leaves. Because this is a biennial, the second year it forms flowers it will begin to die. To insure a constant supply of parsley, it is best to plant two to three times a year. When planting successively, choose different locations each season to allow the soil to host a different variety of plant. This helps keep the soil more fertile and allows for healthier plants. A dressing of compost each spring and fall is about the only care needed. Spray with insecticidal soap and B.T. every 10 days to discourage slugs, snails and dill worms. Italian parsley dries well. Curly parsley and chervil keep better frozen and used in the frozen state—much like dill and chives.

ROSEMARY

Rosemary is best purchased as a nursery plant or taken from cuttings. Plant in the spring or fall 2 feet apart. Upright rosemary can attain a height of 4' – 5' and a diameter of 3'. Rosemary likes a soil on the acidic side, so add lime or fireplace ashes if your soil is alkaline or clay. Rosemary leaves like to be misted daily but the soil needs to remain on the dry side. Too much moisture may bring on root rot or mildew. However, do NOT let the soil dry out completely; this condition will result in instant death. Root rot can be treated fairly successfully with the addition of diatomaceous earth. Mildew can be sprayed with zenob. Every three weeks feed with iron and blood meal or spray with sea kelp. Cut as needed but never more than 1/3 of the plant at a time. Rosemary can sustain a low temperature of 20°F. If the winters are very severe, overwinter in the house or greenhouse or prune back in the fall and mulch heavily with hay or grass clippings.

Most varieties have a small blue flower that nestles among the leaves. Some will bloom all year with a profusion of flowers. Most will bloom twice a year in the spring and fall. There are white varieties and one pink variety to choose from when planning your landscape or herb garden. Upright varieties can be pruned to resemble poodle trees or Christmas trees. The trailing varieties are very useful in hanging baskets, rock gardens or in terraced settings, over topiaries or forming living Easter egg baskets.

SAGE

A perennial: There are many varieties of sage and all can be grown from seed or taken from cuttings. Seeds should be planted in a well watered flat and then put in a fairly dark area and left alone for 5 – 7 days. As soon as the plants are up and the first true leaves are showing, transplant to 4" pots for three – four weeks. These plants will be ready to go outside in the garden. Sage likes sun but not a lot of wind. The soil should be kept on the acidic and dry side. Sage has a tendency to develop root rot and mildew if conditions are too wet or there is high humidity for a long period of time. Work diatomaceous soil around the plant for root rot and spray with zenob for mildew. All plants will need to be replaced after three or four years due to the woody nature of the mature plant. Temperatures of 25°F or below are not tolerated so sage needs to be wintered over in a greenhouse or brought inside during the winter. Golden, broadleaf, variegated and purple sage will reach a height of three feet and a diameter of the same. Common sage has smaller leaves and will only reach a height of one and a half feet and a circumference of about the same. Pineapple sage can reach a height of five to six feet if wintered over in a greenhouse and can be very invasive. However, the beautiful red trumpet-like blossoms that bloom in the spring and fall are worth it. Try several of the varieties to introduce new colors and textures to your landscape or kitchen garden.

SORREL

A perennial: Sorrel seeds can be planted directly into the garden or divisions can be taken in the spring. Allow at least 12" between plants. Sorrel does well in full sun or partial shade. The ground should be slightly acidic and well drained. A dressing of iron and blood meal every month will be welcome and will increase the yield and general health of the plant. Sorrel can reach a height of 2' – 3'. The leaves are most tender and tasty if cut when eight to ten inches long. Never cut more than 1/3 of the plant at a time. Water well and deep during the summer allowing the soil to dry out between waterings. If the plant is not wintered over in a greenhouse or brought indoors in a container, cut the whole plant before the first frost and cover the roots with a good layer of leaves, grass clippings or hay. Mark the area with a name plate and uncover in the early spring. Then begin to look for the small new leaves as your reward for having survived another winter!

TARRAGON

A perennial: Although the "little dragon" is hard to grow, the effort will be grandly rewarded. Propagation is from cuttings, division, or purchased nursery plants, because French tarragon does not produce seed in most climates. Space 12" apart. Tarragon spreads on woody tendrils and sends up branches of leaves to 2 feet. It likes a sunny to partly shaded area and prefers well drained alkaline soil. Tarragon is not tolerant above 90°F and needs protection with shade cloth or remay cloth. Tarragon has to be dormant for a period of time in the winter to insure a healthy plant in the spring. If winters are very cold, cut the tarragon back in the fall and mulch with hay or leaves. Some people take divisions in the fall and place the rooted plant in a plastic bag in the refrigerator for a few days, then placing these plants in a pot for indoor use in the winter. Tarragon needs to be divided and transplanted every two to three years, otherwise the roots have a tendency to strangle the plant. A dressing of sea kelp, fish emulsion or blood meal and iron is necessary every three weeks during the growing season. Root rot is a problem and although the plants like to be kept moist, overwatering is a sure killer.

Note: A substitute plant that looks, smells and tastes like tarragon and is not so difficult to grow is called Mexican Mint Marigold or winter tarragon. It is more heat resistant, can stand damper conditions and is hardier in the winter. Propagation is very easy with cuttings taken most any time of the year or seeds started in the spring. It also has a delightful small yellow flower in the fall that can be added to salads, sauces, garnishes or vegetables. This plant needs to be cut 2" from the ground in the early fall to insure new growth over the winter. It spreads by layering and can be divided in the spring or fall. Most chefs cannot tell the difference between this and the French tarragon, sometimes preferring Mexican Mint Marigold for its longer shelf life.

THYME

A perennial: Thyme grown from seed only produces the creeping variety. Purchase or take cuttings of the varieties you want. Thyme prefers sunny to partial sunny locations but needs to be mulched where summers are quite warm. Lemon thyme is heat sensitive and likes shady areas. The soil should be slightly alkaline and well drained. A light dressing of compost, fish emulsion, blood meal or sea kelp is needed every three to four weeks. Most thyme plants will reach a height of one to one and a half feet and spread about the same. As with all woody stemmed plants, thyme is susceptible to root rot, mildew and fungus and should be kept on the dry side with plenty of air circulation allowed between plants. Never cut more than 1/3 of the plant at a time. Overwintering is advised if winter temperatures fall below 28°F. The plants may be potted and brought into the house or put in a greenhouse. Otherwise, a heavy mulch of hay or grass clippings will be necessary. Because of its woody nature, thyme will need replacing every two to three years. There are whole gardens dedicated to thyme and I hope you will add different varieties each year to your garden and share them with your friends and families.

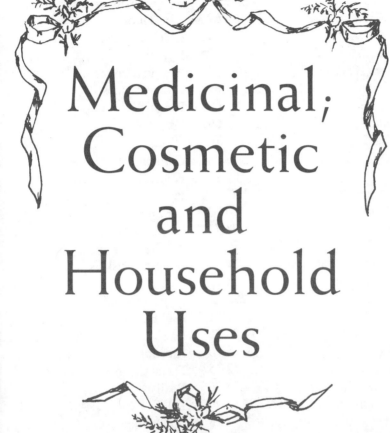

Medicinal,
Cosmetic
and
Household
Uses

MEDICINAL, COSMETIC & OTHER, INDEX

For fully cross-referenced index, see page 83.

GLOSSARY OF TERMS FOR MEDICINAL & COSMETIC USES:

Herbal Teas: Herbal teas are made by pouring 1 cup boiling water over 2 ounces of fresh herbs or 1 ounce of dried herb. Let steep 15 minutes; strain before drinking. Teas should be taken at least 3 times a day. Teas are used in the preparation for fomentations.

Decoction: A stronger tea made by boiling the herbs in the water for 15 minutes. Be sure and cover the pan. Roots and bark are used also. Decoctions can be distilled for an even stronger solution. Decoctions can also be used as the basis for stocks in soups, stews, and rice dishes.

Tincture: 4 ounces of dried herbs that have been reduced to a powder by grinding in a mortar and pestle are added to 1 pint of vodka or brandy in a mason-like jar with a tight lid. Place jar in a sunny window or warm area and let stand for two weeks. Strain through muslin or cheesecloth. Use 5 – 20 drops per day depending upon severity or recommendation. Stronger tinctures can be made by adding more powdered herbs to the alcohol.

Extract: A tincture that has been distilled, thereby making a stronger solution.

Syrup: Slowly cook 1 cup of sugar to 1 cup of herbal decoction until the liquid is reduced to a syrupy consistency. This will last in the refrigerator indefinitely.

Electuaries: Made by blending a combination of dried or powdered herbs in enough honey to make a paste. This may be spooned out and taken as needed. Keep refrigerated.

Poultice: Soak muslin or cheesecloth in a decoction, place over the infected area and wrap with a bandage or adhesive. Replace at least 2 – 3 times daily.

Plaster: Dried herbs are added to enough flour and water to form a paste. Apply with muslin or cheesecloth and secure with a bandage.

Fomentation: Soak muslin or cheesecloth in hot herbal tea, wringing out the excess, and applying to the affected area. Reapply with the warm tea as soon as the cloth cools.

Herbal Bath: Made by pouring 2 cups of herbal tea into a bathtub of water or a muslin bag containing 1/2 cup fresh or dried herbs may be hung over the faucet while the bathtub is filling.

Herbal Oil: 1 cup of leaves, bark or root to 1 cup of oil in a wide mouth jar. Place the jar in a sunny window for 2 – 3 weeks, decant, strain into bottles. Keep out of direct sunlight.

Salves: Put 1/2 ounce of herbal oil in 1 cup of water. Simmer for 20 minutes, strain through cheesecloth or muslin into another pan and repeat these steps until there are only 2 ounces left. Add 2 ounces of olive oil and simmer until all the water has evaporated. Add 1/8 teaspoon tincture of benzoin and 1 ounce of beeswax. The salve may be stored in a small jar and kept in a cool place. Will keep fresh for 6 months.

MEDICINAL

Some recommended remedies for various conditions are presented here. They are suggestions from my own experience and from others and are not meant to take the place of a physician's advice or counsel. If a chronic condition persists, professional medical advice should be sought. There are many holistic doctors that could be contacted through any physician referral network.

Basil:
• High fevers of over 104°F may be lowered by drinking basil tea 3 – 5 times a day, or until fever begins to subside.

• Upset stomachs caused by gas or tension can be relieved by drinking basil tea.

• Wasp and bee sting poison is drawn out by applying crushed basil leaves to the sting for 15 minutes.

Dill:
• Colic responds well to a dill tea that has been diluted by half.

• Stomach cramps in adults can be alleviated by drinking dill tea.

• Hyperactivity or restlessness can be helped by drinking a tea made from dill seeds. Use 1 teaspoon dill seeds to 1 cup water.

• Sleep can be induced by warming dill seeds, wrapping them up in a cloth and laying them beside your head.

• Hiccups can be cured by putting dill seeds in warm red wine. Let steep for 10 minutes before drinking. (About 1/2 teaspoon dill seeds per cup of warm red wine.)

Edible flowers:
• First degree burns can be soothed and healed by applying a fomentation of sage or marigold flowers.

• Eyestrain can be eased by bathing the eyes in borage tea.

• Stress due to nerves is thought to respond well to the aroma of lavender.

• Aching muscles respond to equal parts of marigold juice and vinegar added to the bath water.

• Warts, callouses and corns can be diminished or eliminated by applying a marigold poultice to them. Use 2 – 3 times a day until gone.

Marigold:
• Bruises, burns and stings will benefit from a poultice of marigold flowers.

• Sunburns will cool and heal faster if marigold oil is applied to the skin.

Marjoram:
• Insomnia or sleeplessness can be alleviated when marjoram leaves are made into a pillow or sachet and laid by your head.

• Head colds and sore muscles can be helped by drinking marjoram tea.

• Liver and spleen can be cleansed by drinking a decoction made from marjoram.

• Bruises are healed by rubbing a marjoram salve on them.

• Earaches or ringing in the ear is reported to be helped by putting two drops of marjoram oil in the ear.

• Tension headaches can be relieved by drinking marjoram tea.

Mint:
• Digestion can be aided by drinking a cup of peppermint tea or by chewing some peppermint leaves.

• Breath is freshened by chewing spearmint leaves.

• Joint and muscle pain is greatly lessened by applying peppermint ointment or salve.

• Liver and gall bladder is said to be stimulated by drinking peppermint tea. Drink 3 – 5 cups a day.

• Appetites improve if a cup of peppermint tea is taken before meals.

• Oxygen and blood flow can be stimulated by drinking a cup of peppermint or lemon mint tea. It cleanses the blood and raises the body's temperature.

Oregano:
• Chest colds or chronic coughs respond well to oregano tea.

• Swelling and pain in the joints can be alleviated by applying a poultice of oregano oil.

Parsley— curly:
• Bladder and urinary infections can be prevented and/or dramatically helped by drinking parsley tea several times a day. Do not continue for more than two weeks. Pregnant women should not drink parsley tea.

• Eye irritation due to strain or environmental pollution can be soothed by using parsley tea as a wash.

• Kidney stones are reputed to be dissolved or diminished by drinking parsley tea.

• Arteriosclerosis may diminish by drinking parsley tea that has a clove of garlic added to it.

• Bursitis can be helped by drinking parsley tea 3 – 4 times a day.

Rosemary:
• Painful cramping due to menstruation can be eased by drinking rosemary tea.

• Rheumatic pain due to swelling of joints is diminished by rubbing the area with rosemary salve or ointment.

• Energy is enhanced when rosemary tea is taken.

• Tired and sore muscles due to exercise and strain will be soothed and relaxed by adding 2 cups of rosemary tea to bath water.

• Migraine headaches often diminish or disappear when rosemary tea is taken.

Sage:
• Cleansing the body of toxins can be accomplished by drinking sage tea.

• Heavy periods are said to be lessened by drinking sage tea.

• Sore throats and hoarseness are soothed and healed with sage tea.

• Ulcers in the mouth or throat are diminished by gargling with sage tea.

• Hot flashes are thought to be reduced or lightened by drinking sage tea.

• Baldness is said to be prevented by preparing a rosemary and sage decoction. Use as a rinse, massaging in well, and do not wash out. Repeat at least 3 times a week.

• Depression can be relieved by drinking sage tea.

Thyme:
• Lung congestion due to colds can be broken up by drinking thyme tea.

• Asthma relief is provided by taking thyme as an electuary or syrup.

• Congestion headaches respond to thyme tea.

COSMETIC USES FOR FACE AND BODY

Herbs have long been used to enhance, rejuvenate, cleanse, perfume, beautify and adorn the human body. Their fragrance as well as their chemicals can relax, stimulate, soothe, smooth, and color. These are just a few suggestions from collected knowledge.

Basil:
• Skin freshener and tonic: Use basil tea as a wash.

Dill:
• Breath freshener: Chew dill seeds.

• Hiccups stop when dill tea is drunk.

Lavender:
• Hairwash: Use a lavender decoction as a hair conditioner and restorer. Massage into the scalp and leave on. (See *Sage* under *Medicinal Suggestions.*)

• Rejuvenation: Add two cups of tea or decoction to the bath water.

Marigold:
• Eyewash: Use marigold tea made from the petals to relieve redness and puffiness.

• Moisturizer: Marigold salve or ointment leaves the skin smooth, clear and very moist.

Marjoram:
• Massage Oil: Use as an oil to warm, soothe and relax tired muscles and over-exposed or sunburned skin.

• Perfume Oil: Marjoram oil can be added to other perfumes to enhance their staying power.

Mint:
• Toner: Use the tea to wake up or energize and stimulate the complexion. Peppermint or lemon mint may be used.

• Rejuvenate: Use peppermint oil to massage tired bodies back to life. Especially refreshing in the summer.

Parsley:
• Freckles: Use parsley juice twice a day on the freckles until they fade away.
• Astringent: Use curly parsley tea as a wash to clear up and tighten the skin.
• Hair rinse: Parsley tea is a great hair tonic for cleaner, healthier hair.

Rosemary:
• Dandruff: Use rosemary tea combined with thyme tea as a rinse. Apply to dry or wet hair. Leave on for 30 minutes or longer — no need to rinse.
• Hair restorer: Rosemary oil massaged into the scalp and left on for 45 minutes will stimulate the scalp and hair follicles.
• Cleanser: Use the tea as a facial cleanser to increase blood flow to the face.
• Bath: Rosemary tea added to a warm bath will soothe and relax the muscles and bring a healthy sheen to the skin.
• Massage: Rosemary oil is a deep muscle relaxant, improving circulation through increased blood flow.

Sage:
• Dye: Sage tea applied to dark hair, will color the gray and leave the hair shining and very manageable. For best results, use on dry hair.
• Teeth: Use a sage leaf to rub across your teeth to whiten and clean.

Thyme:
• Dandruff: Mixed in equal parts with rosemary tea used as a hair rinse.

OTHER USES

Using herbs to brighten and freshen each room in your home will extend the benefits of your garden all year round. Sharing your garden's treasures with others is a pleasure and a double blessing. Following are some suggestions for your home and for novel and appreciated remembrances for others.

Basil:
• In potpourris, sachets and wreaths, the clove and minty aromas associated with the different varieties add depth and interest.

Opal basil:
• Especially beautiful added to floral arrangements or as a wreath all by itself. Include some recipe suggestions if giving one as a gift.

Chives:
• The flowers of both garlic and regular chives are very beautiful tucked into fresh or dried floral arrangements.

• Add them to oils and vinegars that have already been decanted.

• Chive flowers dry very nicely and can be glued onto dried wreaths.

Dill:
• The flowering heads are used in country bouquets.

• Dill heads are always used in pickling.

• Try a whole dill head on an open sandwich for added color and taste.

Edible flowers:
• Make a wreath using only these fresh flowers for an edible centerpiece. If taken as a gift to a friend, include some recipes with the card.

• Edible flowers dropped into ice cube trays that are filled with bottled water can be used in cold drinks or in punch bowls.

• Fresh or candied, they may be used to decorate cakes, muffins and puddings and tea cakes.

• For a festive summertime outing, make a garland of fresh flowers for your straw hat. Pin to ribbon and tie around the crown of the hat.

Lavender:
• The long spires with or without flowers make a wonderful and aromatic arrangement for any room in the house.

• Make a sachet out of dried leaves and flowers as part of a decorative wrapping on the outside of a gift.

• Make a lavender water—use the recipe for a tea—and give to a friend who needs some cheering up. Makes a refreshing toner, especially in the summer.

• Add the dried flowers to potpourri.

• Bundle old or dried branches together and add to the fireplace in the winter. This releases a lovely spring-like aroma throughout the room.

• At Christmas time, a wreath made exclusively of lavender is beautiful over the mantle or on the door. These make very attractive and distinctive gifts.

Marjoram:
• A scented candle made from melted paraffin and marjoram oil will soothe and calm the whole household.

• Make a "sleep" pillow using dried marjoram and any pretty piece of fabric. These are placed by the sleeper's head or put inside a regular pillow. These make great baby shower gifts.

• Fresh marjoram put in a muslin bag and hung over the faucet in the bath will soothe frayed nerves.

Mint:
• The fragrance of other herbs is enhanced when mint is added to potpourris.

• A jug of spearmint or lemon mint tea taken as your contribution to the next pot luck supper will be a welcome change of beverage.

• Hanging baskets will freshen and rejuvenate all who sit by them.

• Lemon or spearmint tea added to the bath water will refresh and invigorate.

Oregano:
• The longer stems of the upright oregano make a good base for a dried wreath. Add the shorter creeping oregano as a filler along with other favorite culinary herbs.

• The mauve flowers of the creeping oregano are beautiful fresh or dried and are a very attractive addition to bouquets.

• Because oregano is used in so many Mexican and Mediterranean recipes, a jar filled with fresh dried leaves makes a wonderful bread and butter gift.

• Creeping oregano can be trained as topiaries and used as gifts or "living" centerpieces.

Parsley:
• Use the long stalks of Italian flat leaf parsley in arrangements.

• The curly or chervil varieties work nicely in wreaths.

• Soft floral forms can be covered with curly parsley or chervil and used around punch bowls, etc. Soak the form in water to keep the parsley fresher longer.

Rosemary:
• A lovely aromatic addition to fresh or dried arrangements.

• Rosemary makes a beautiful wreath all by itself. Tie a seasonal ribbon at the bottom to add color.

• Trailing rosemary can be trained as living Easter egg baskets by attaching a wire handle to a pot and tying the new growth to the handles. Trim back excess branches. Use as centerpieces or give as gifts.

• The upright varieties can be pruned as Christmas trees or "poodle" trees. (This takes a number of years, so be patient.)

• Tie bundles of rosemary stems together as faggots for the fireplace in the winter.

Sage:
• Because of its dusty appearance and vivid blue or pink flowers, sage is a welcome addition to dried and fresh arrangements.

• Purple, variegated and tricolor all lend important contrasts and should be remembered when decorating wreaths.

Tarragon:
• A bottle of freshly made tarragon vinegar is a welcome housewarming gift.

Thyme:
• Whole wreaths can be made up of several different kinds of thyme; include recipes if giving one as a gift.

• A bottle of thyme wine makes a great gift for older people or someone who needs a boost to their energy level.

Notes:

BIBLIOGRAPHY AND RESOURCES

Back, Philippa, *The Illustrated Herbal*, New York, Crown Publishing, Inc., 1987.

Bianchini, Francesco and Corbetta, *The Complete Book of Health Plants*, New York; Crescent Books, 1975.

Boxer, Arabella, and Philippa Back, *The Herb Book*, London; Octopus Books, 1980.

Culpepper, Nicholas, *Culpepper's Complete Herbal*, Secaucus, New Jersey; Chartwell Books, Inc., 1985.

Genders, Roy, *Cosmetic, A Guide to Natural Beauty from the Earth*, New York: Alfred van der Marck Editions, 1985.

Gordon, Lesley, *A Country Herbal*, New York; Gallery Books, 1980.

Grieve, Mrs. M., *A Modern Herbal, 2 Vol.*, New York; Dover Publications, 1971.

Kowalchik, Claire and William H. Hylton, *Rodale's Illustrated Encyclopedia of Herbs*, Emmaus, Pennsylvania; Rodale Press, 1987.

Lust, John, *The Herb Book New York*; B. Lust Publications, 1974.

Lust, John N.D., and Michael Tierra, C.A., O.M.D., *The Natural Remedy Bible*, New York; Pocket Books, 1990.

Mabey, Richard, *The New Age Herbalist*, New York, Macmillan Publishing Company, 1988.

Ohrbach, Barbara M., *The Scented Room*, New York; Clarkson N. Potter, Inc., 1986.

Ohrbach, Barbara M., *A Token of Friendship*, New York; Clarkson N. Potter, Inc., 1987.

Rechelbacher, Horst, *Rejuvenation: A Wellness Guide for Women and Men*, Vermont; Healing Arts Press, 1989.

Stuart, Malcolm, Ed., *The Encyclopedia of Herbs and Herbalism*, New York; Crescent Books, 1981.

Tolley, Emelie, and Chris Meak, *Herbs, Gardens, Decorations, and Recipes*, New York; Clarkson N. Potter, 1986.

The Herb Purveyor Price List

305-278-7321 fax • Collect 305-278-7010

One 16-ounce amber jar will take 1 to 1 1/2 lbs. of herbs for oils and vinegars.
One 12" wreath requires 4 to 6 lbs. of fresh herbs.

Arugula	$ 7.00	Tarragon	$ 18.00
Basil	8.00	Thyme	12.00
Chives	15.00	Sorrel	10.00
Chervil	18.00	Edible flowers	12.00
Dill	6.50	Lemon thyme	12.00
Marjoram	10.00	Ojo Sante	16.00
Mint	6.00	Epizote	8.00
Oregano	10.00	Italian parsely	5.00
Rosemary	11.00	Bay leaves	15.00
Sage	11.50	Lavender	12.00

All prices are by the pound. Herbs are cut, packed and shipped the day of the order and delivered to you tomorrow. All herbs are shipped in protected, cooled boxes that insure the freshness and quality of the herbs. Most of the herbs are organically grown and your satisfaction is guaranteed. I appreciate the opportunity of sharing these herbs and will do all in my power to deliver the finest quality, most flavorful herbs available anywhere.

Respectfully,

Barbara Scoggins

Barbara Scoggins Frush, Owner

NOTE:
❖ *Minimum order of 8 lbs. required*   ❖ *Orders are C.O.D.*
❖ *Add $7.50 for postage & handling*

INDEX

Notes:

To order additional copies, make checks payable to:
Father & Son Publishing, Inc. and mail to:
4909 North Monroe Street • Tallahassee, Florida 32303

Please send me_____ copies of **The Herb Cookery** @ $9.95 plus $3.00
each for postage and handling. Florida residents add 7% sales tax.
Enclosed is my check or money order for $_____

Name _____

Address _____

City_____ State _____ Zip _____

Mastercard/Visa Card#_____

Exp.date _____ Signature _____

To order additional copies, make checks payable to:
Father & Son Publishing, Inc. and mail to:
4909 North Monroe Street • Tallahassee, Florida 32303

Please send me_____ copies of **The Herb Cookery** @ $9.95 plus $3.00
each for postage and handling. Florida residents add 7% sales tax.
Enclosed is my check or money order for $_____

Name _____

Address _____

City _____ State _____ Zip _____

Mastercard/Visa Card#_____

Exp.date _____ Signature _____

To order additional copies, make checks payable to:
Father & Son Publishing, Inc. and mail to:
4909 North Monroe Street • Tallahassee, Florida 32303

Please send me_____ copies of **The Herb Cookery** @ $9.95 plus $3.00
each for postage and handling. Florida residents add 7% sales tax.
Enclosed is my check or money order for $_____

Name _____

Address _____

City _____ State _____ Zip _____

Mastercard/Visa Card#_____

Exp.date _____ Signature _____

Remember, these books make great gifts. Send one to a friend today!
Gift wrap and direct ship to your friend for only $1.00 additional.

Notes: